DID I REALLY DO THAT?
HOW TO REALISE YOUR DREAMS.

Chapter One
"FROM A HUMBLE BEGINNING"

I hope that after you have read this chapter, it will make you realise that with determination and my help, you will be able to workout how to change your life and make some of your dreams come true. I know that I am no better than anyone else but perhaps a little bit different.

Is it that what makes us all the individuals that we are? Probably my experiences shaped my character.

I was born in Balham at a very tender age to a not very wealthy family living in a council house. Our family name was Hutton. Like all youngsters I got up to a lot of mischief and defied my Mother frequently. I was told every day, "You will never be as clever as your Father or your Sister". So to be even more disobedient I left off trying.

During the Second World War of 1938 to 1945, My Father divorced my Mother and although I was only 5 years old at the time, I remember very clearly the day the papers arrived.

With no Father to correct me, all the discipline came from one direction: **my Mother**.

On a few occasions when Mum was scared for our survival;

Photo of me with Auntie Ethel 1938

Dad and his two daughters

my sister and I were dutifully put on a train with the obligatory label attached to a button hole of our coat plus the gas mask on a long string around our necks and sent off to a chicken farm somewhere in Yorkshire. This next bit is exactly true. The farmer and his wife were called Mr. and Mrs. Bantam. I have never forgotten their name, but have never seen them since the days of the war. Life for us there was fun and exciting, living on a farm in the countryside, with no bombs or air raid warnings or having to run to a shelter late at night. This was all very different from Balham in London where we lived. Every morning, Mrs. Bantam would take both of us by the hand to the chicken coups to see if there was an egg each for breakfast. Again I can still remember that feeling of excitement at seeing real live chickens doing what chickens do. We had to sing *"Hey little hen, when, when, when will you lay me an egg for my tea"*? We were both told that the chickens would not lay an egg unless we sang this song. It was some years later that I was at last convinced that this was not so.

Mum, Maureen and myself.

Youth and naivety are wonderful and it would be such a shame to burst the bubble.

After some time our Mum became very lonely without her children and brought us back home to Balham for a time. Unfortunately the bombs were getting nearer, and every night we lost all our windows. As we had no Anderson shelter we slept in a hammock in the coal cellar, with all the coal, I hasten to add. It was very dirty, stuffy and smelly, but it was safer than hiding under the dining room table. Sometimes I used to shelter behind my doll's pram until Mum found out and clipped me round the ear for being stupid.

Our Father became very agitated about our safety and insisted that we went to live with his Mother, our Granny Hutton, in Tadcaster Yorkshire.

Her cottage was opposite John Smiths Brewery which is still there and flourishing. To this day I cannot stand the smell of hops. During my time there as a kid during the war, the cottage consisted of a scullery with a black range for heating water and for cooking, a cream butler sink with one cold tap and gas light downstairs. The bedrooms were up a flight of stairs with no gas light just a candle in a holder. Washing facilities were a marble top washstand with a china bowl and pitcher filled with cold water. These items today are a cherished possession and have a collectors' antique value of anything up to £400.00

During the night if you needed the toilet facilities, good use was made of the china potty hidden under the bed, known as a gazunder, because it "goes under the bed". These too have a value, usually more so when empty. During the day the toilet facilities were much more up market.

Going out t' backdoor and in't' yard there was a neat row of toilets for the occupants of the cottages. These consisted of green painted wooden doors that were not full sized, which enabled you to see which ones were occupied or vacant by either male or

top left; Dad in his Army uniform.
Below right; The old cooking range

4

female. If you use your imagination here you can very soon work out how to differentiate between the sexes. There was a proper toilet with a high level cistern and a piece of rusty chain complete with rubber handle, which, as they now would say, "Needs some renovation". No electricity, just a candle, or if you were lucky, a torch to see where you were going. The natural wild life inhabited these toilets. As a small child I was scared of spiders that always seemed to come down on my legs whilst I was sitting on the loo.

If the weather was bad, I was made to put on a pair of wellies, a mackintosh, thick coat, hat and gloves, just to answer a call of nature. Things have improved, haven't they?

It was my job once a week to cut the newspapers into squares, use a meat skewer, and bore a hole into one corner through which I would thread hairy string. All of this was ceremoniously hang on a nail and labelled toilet paper. This would now be classed as being very GREEN.

From time to time our Grandma entertained the American soldiers in her parlour, during which time we were not allowed in. The up side was, we got a regular piece of chocolate. This was a real treat.

In Tadcaster there is a dam crossing the River Wharfe, which my father told me that he used to walk all the way across without falling in. I thought, anything he can do, so can I. I was half way across when I slipped on all the slimy weeds and fell into the river. As I could not swim, all I remember is darkness as the water closed over my head. Fortunately for me someone had seen me go in and dived in to rescue me. I eventually came too lying on the grassy bank with my Mother anxiously looking down at me. She was very cross for two reasons; I had spoilt my clothes, and she actually said, *"If you ever do anything as dangerous as that again I'll kill you"*. I received quite a large slap and was dragged home, wet, bedraggled, cold and unhappy. Oh well, I thought, what an achievement.

I have in recent years been back to look at the dam, it is still there but gaining access is no longer available.

Tadcaster Bridge over the R. Wharfe

5

Tadcaster brewery with its chimney

The very tall chimney which was visible from the back yard belonged to the Brewery and they wanted it knocked down. It was very close to all the cottages so all day long for many weeks, two men sat astride the top of the chimney and knocked the bricks into the centre, whilst they slowly inched their way around the very top until finally one day the chimney was no more.

Everyone of a certain age will remember Friday night as bath night. In Tadcaster there was no bathroom, so Friday night was a major expedition. Plenty of cast iron pots were put on the black coal fired range to heat some water, which took hours. When this was ready the bungalow bath was brought in from the yard and placed ont' scullery floor in front of t' range. There was never enough water, not even enough to cover ones possibilities and no privacy, as, after all, this would take place in the kitchen next to the back door through which various family members would walk from time to time. Oh well, I thought, you are young and at the moment you do not have a lot to hide.

Things became a bit strained living with our paternal Grandma, so we came back down South. During our time up north our home had received a direct hit and we lost almost everything, except the clothes we stood up in. During the day we went to see the devastation and what was left of our home. It was completely flattened. The only thing left standing was the front door. We borrowed a wheelbarrow and started rummaging for any of our belongings. We found quite a bit of coal which would help us keep warm and the second item was our wireless, which when dusted and cleaned and switched on was still working. It was another 10 years before we needed to buy a new one. They don't make 'em like that anymore do they?

We now had no home and nowhere to live, but at a time like this, family will always step in. We at last moved in with our Maternal Grandmother and Grandfather who lived behind the cinema in Morden Surrey. As a child this was not too much of a trauma, but for Mum, Granny and Grand Dad as you can imagine it was quite an upheaval to suddenly have 3 extra people living in your house, and not knowing for how long. We were still suffering from every night bombing raids; so on each of these occasions we spent the night in the Anderson shelter in Granddads' vegetable patch at the bottom of his very long garden. One night upon arriving in the shelter I discovered that my teddy bear was still in the house. As this would be IMPOSSIBLE for me to sleep without him, when Mum was distracted I left the shelter, ran up the long garden path into the back door, ran upstairs, found my teddy bear, ran downstairs to the back door ready to run the gauntlet to the shelter. By this time my Mum had noticed that I was absent and she was standing in the shelter doorway screaming at me.

V2 Rocket

As I stepped out of the house I heard a very familiar sound overhead, yes, you've guessed, it was a V2 rocket with flames at the rear. I already knew from past experience, that all the while you can hear the noise and see the flames you are safe. The danger would come when all went quiet. I decided to run to the shelter whilst this THING followed my flight path.

I dived headlong into the shelter, Mum clipped me around the ear, the door was slammed shut and sand bagged.

The rocket landed at the very end of the garden and exploded. Fortunately no one was killed or even hurt. The only damage being, all the dirt was blown from the roof of the shelter plus some of Granddad's vegetables were no longer fit for human consumption. Lastly my right ear was sore from the clout I had received earlier. (But that gets better very quickly).

Finally in 1945 the war came to an end and those of you who can remember this will know how much celebration took place.

Many years after the war ended, Granny's neighbour had a problem with subsidence and suitable workmen were called in to investigate. To everyone's horror and disbelief there was a German bomb buried in the garden, still live and moving towards the house, which by now everyone knew why the house was suffering from subsidence. We were all evacuated for the day to Morden cinema and given free showings of many films, followed by food and drink. As youngsters this was called an adventure.

The bomb disposal squad were called in and on uncovering it completely, the offending object was defused and made safe. We were all allowed to come back to watch an enormous crane position itself in the road whilst the long arm came over the top of the house, the bomb was attached with chains and hooks and lifted ceremoniously over the roof of the house, loaded onto a lorry and driven away. As kids, this was so exciting and was talked about at school for weeks. I can even remember bragging to my mates that "I had taken part in defusing an enemy bomb, helping to save lives and watched it taken away". Oh well, kids are wicked and untruthful at times. This was called COLOURING THE TRUTH.

13 years old

By the age of eight and the War was over, I was a Tom Boy and looking for adventures and excitements. This took the form of climbing trees, the taller and more difficult the better. Unfortunately this meant that on many occasions my clothes were not only dirty but usually torn, which prompted yet another beating from Mum. Rationing was still in force so buying new clothes was almost out of the question, as the money we had, was spent on more important things like food. You would be surprised how good your clothes can look if darned carefully.

I passed my 11 plus to a Grammar school where I proved that I was not good academically, but shone at gymnastics, acrobatics and sport of all kinds. I could not only run very fast, which my Mother said was due to the fact that my feet were size 8, but I was very good at high jump. I even had the privilege of my own trainer at the local running track.

My class mates would tease me about the size of my feet. When someone came into the classroom and let the door slam, everyone would pretend to pick up my feet and carefully move them out of the way of the door, even if I was sitting at the other end of the classroom.

After the war ended rationing was still in force including clothing and shoes. One afternoon during school time our teacher drew two chalk lines on the wooden floor and then asked all the class members to remove their shoes, place their heel on the first line and if their toe went over the second line they would be entitled to extra shoe coupons. As I was the youngest participant I was told by the teacher that it was a waste of time for me to measure my foot. When she finally left the classroom I decided

8

to measure my foot just to prove her wrong. Guess what my foot went way over the chalk mark much to everyone's surprise. My Mother was delighted as this meant extra clothing coupons.

At the age of eleven I broke all records in England, Wales and Scotland for high jump by clearing 4 feet 6 inches. WOW! I wonder what the record is today?

I was now 13 and started to learn to play a game called Korfball. The word KORF is Dutch for basket, and by the age of 16, I was playing for England. Not really very important as not a lot of people know of the game.

Throughout my younger days, Mum was very physically violent. At the time I thought this was due to the trauma of being bombed every night, sustaining damage to our house, plus the terror that went with it. Being very fed up with the regular beatings from my Mother, one day I retaliated and broke her thumb in the fight. After this episode she never laid another finger on me in temper, not even a thumb.

I was beginning to learn to stand up for myself. From that day on I vowed that no one would ever knock me down again and I would start to change my life.

Ann, Korfball player on left

By the age of sixteen and a half I left the Grammar school without any qualifications to speak of, having as I thought, finished my education. How to earn my living was a concern. Harrods was my first introduction to the big outdoor world of high finance. I genuinely believed that the only way I was accepted was when asked which school did you go to, in my best accent I could manage I said, "Actually it was Rosa Bassett School for young ladies". If I had said it was Stretum (Streatham) Grammar I think Woolworths would have been my destination.

I worked in the children's wear department ages 2 to 7 for 3 very happy years. I took a course of elocution lessons to enable me to speak without too much of my cockney showing through. I was taught window dressing, people skills and a telephone manner. Always smile when you answer the phone and greet the caller, I was taught. Victor Borge taught me that no two people can continue to punch each other whilst smiling, and that a smile is the shortest distance between two people. If only more of us could live by this suggestion. I was quickly learning that if you pretend you have knowledge, providing you are flamboyant enough at the time, you will be believed and you can make great strides forward. I finally left Harrods as I was getting fed up with toffee nosed people who had money and thought that as I, a mere shop assistant was at the lower end of the human chain.

9

So, what to do now? My Father suggested that a job in a bank would be more financially beneficial. So with nerves and trepidation I attended an interview to be accepted to work at Lloyds Bank Southwark. I was immediately sent to their college, and much to my surprise, I became the top banking student for that year. WOW!

I was at last beginning to believe that I did have some brains, although they had been dormant for some time and that my Mum wasn't always right. I needed to learn to be able to earn.

After just 2 years I left the Bank, took a CHANCE and married an Ironmonger of the same name with a family business of 7 Hardware shops, an Interflora Florist and a lawn mower engineering workshop. Later, together, we started our own Wholesale Company where we bought goods for over 60 other Ironmongers in the Surrey area, to be able to compete with the Big Boys of the day.

One of the hardware shops owned by Henry Chance Ltd.

Ann wearing her Presidential chain of office with wooden spoon.

10

I then decided to expand my knowledge and after a few years study became a professional lady Ironmonger and an Interflora florist. My knowledge of lawn mower repairs are very sketchy; in fact I know nothing at all. I became the first and ever lady President of the London & Southern Counties Ironmongers Association, (what a mouthful) and served on the Board of Management of the British Hardware Federation. I bet you are Impressed. Mind you not many people have ever heard of these two associations. But c'est la vie.)

By now I was the proud possessor of 2 sons, 1 dog, 6 puppies and like all Mums one salary. Being an Employer and not an Employee was very hard to come to terms with. I wanted to convince our staff that I was the same as all of them except my name being over the door of the shops. This is how I came to write funny odes about work and Ironmongers, which realised my aim in letting the staff see that after all I was only human. (Read book 2 for more odes. Title: Odes of a Lifetime or some poems wot I 'ave writ)

My husband now had become a Rotarian, and I, an Inner Wheel member. In these capacities we spent many happy hard working hours raising money for people in our community who were less fortunate than ourselves.

One episode will live forever in my thoughts and that was my parachute jump dressed as Wonder Woman, my eldest son as Robin, a Rotarian as Batman and the newspapers sent Superman disguised as Clark Kent. This feat took place at Headcorn where £2,500 was raised. We worked together with the local Doctors and Nurses and Leonard Cheshire DFC and bar and started our own Care at Home Service for physically disabled adults.

My second memorable feat was not only sharing a dressing room with Cardew Robinson the Cad, but actually performing alongside him. This show raised enough money to buy no less than three electric carts in bright red for disabled children. The organisation was known as The Ewell Children's Aid Society.

From a poor and shaky start in life, I was realising some of my dreams, through hard work, determination and sheer bloody mindedness. Beneath me somewhere was a talent I was just beginning to

My Sons. Ian above and Keith.

11

NEWS

93 Benhill Road, Sutton, Surrey, SM1 3RR
Telephone: 01-661 2221

On your bike

Fund raising for
very worthy causes.
I always enjoyed
getting up to all
sorts of pranks for
raising funds.
Here you see me on
a bicycle made for...
how many?
And of course as
Wonder Woman
with son Ian as
Robin, a fellow
Rotarian as Batman
and of course the
local press sent
along Superman
disguised as Clark
Kent. Here you see
us getting used to
heights ready for
our parachute jump
for real..see over,
and we all landed
the right way up
safely.

12

find. I was able to communicate with people, share many troubles and at the same time make people laugh. I even attended evening classes to study British Sign Language for the deaf. This was the way forward to enable me to talk to some of my hard of hearing and totally deaf customers.

I practised most every day and played tunes for the neighbours who would My husband was able to play a musical instrument so I decided to learn to play the saxophone. My neighbours would shout over the fence, "We recognised that one". Our Border collie was not so accommodating; she would sit beside me, throw her head back like a wolf and howl. Having to a degree mastered the saxophone; I became over confident and wanted to learn to play different instruments. Whilst on holiday in Spain I bought myself a very cheap six string guitar and bought a book for idiots on "How to play". I can now proudly boast that I can play the saxophone the guitar, the descant, treble and base recorder, comb and paper and split peas in an empty fairy liquid bottle, most of the aforementioned quite badly.

Nevertheless having mastered the intricacies of music, I now perform a one woman show, where I play the guitar, sing, (very badly) tell stories, jokes and get my audience singing and having fun, where everyone goes home laughing and happy. It gives me a lovely feeling of warmth to be able to help people partake in this type of fun.

In 1987, our family businesses became unprofitable and we found ourselves in financial difficulties. Our two sons were now adults and could manage for themselves, so with sadness we had to cut our losses, sell the family businesses and our large house. We firstly moved into a rented flat, then a terraced house, downsized everything, paid off our creditors and tried to find another way to earn a living. Life was now decidedly different and extremely difficult. But, as they say, "We British are made of sterner stuff and we will survive".

At this time, our youngest son went into business with a partner and opened a shop where he not only designed kitchens, bedrooms and bathrooms but had the qualifications to be a fitter of the above. As I was still trying to find a new type of employment he asked me to help with his business. I taught him how to a run a business and he taught me how to use a computer and the most difficult thing for a woman; how to measure accurately. My youngest son had taught me a very valuable lesson. Unfortunately during the recession in the 1980's his business collapsed and I was again unemployed at a very mature age.

Our eldest son was now a highly qualified aeronautical engineer working at Gatwick airport for firstly British Airways and then he moved up the ladder to become an employee of Delta airlines. This gives a Mum a lovely warm feeling to know how clever your sons are.

I felt fairly comfortable that both our boys would be now self sufficient and could stand on their own two feet.

I was not going to be beaten again, so in my mid 50's I embarked on another new career. After two years study, whilst working with physically disabled adults I gained my N.V.Q grade 3 in long term supportive care and was given a title of "Senior Care Attendant".

My days were very long, some times 13 hours working with 14 clients. The up side was that I was slowly becoming more financially stable as the days and weeks went by.

Then tragedy struck again our Father died at the age of 68 from a stroke followed by a heart attack. My sister and I inherited a property and his shares, of which there were quite a few. His job was in Wall Street London buying and selling shares for the more affluent folks of his time. He was in his field very well known not only for his skill in the Stock Market but as a communist writing under a pseudonym for The Daily Star. He obviously had to keep his identity secret due to whom he was working for and the type of job he was doing. He wrote under the name of William Mennell. In my younger days I found it very exciting to have a Father who was IN DISGUISE and doing something that was regarded as almost illegal. My Dad grew up in Tadcaster, Yorkshire. His Father was a skilled mechanic. At the age of 16

Myself and Dad

he moved to London and started work in the financial sector. He had seen the depression of the 20's -30's, much of his time was spent helping charities with their financial investments.

After WW2 he joined the staff of Vanderfelt and Company. His earlier experience led him to believe that the capitalist system would fail even though he worked at the heart of it. He campaigned for 'Ban the Bomb' under the slogan 'Homes not Horror'. He was actively involved in speaking out against high rents and bad housing, in fact his life was taken over by his trade union work. He was chairman of the Acton Branch and was a delegate to the National Conference of the Clerical and Administration Workers Union. He was an honest man and would not tolerate any form of trickery. His first book was 'Tax dodging by the Rich', which was published in the Daily Worker under the pseudonym of William Mennell. Dad had several books published and they are still studied as part of economic history in the world libraries today. He wrote his last book entitled 'Calculating' with his wife Joyce who was a maths teacher.

My Dad believed in Socialism and that this would open up possibilities of solving the problems of feeding the worlds population and improving the lot of the desperately deprived. Privilege through wealth would disappear with everyone enjoying a more satisfactory way of life. He was a modest gentleman and had a great sense of humour. I loved my Dad and still miss him today.

One of Dads books still available today

15

Chapter Two

"LOOKING AHEAD"

My next challenge was beginning to rear its head. Since taking part in the parachute jump, there was something infectious about wanting to learn to fly. With just over two and a half years training I gained my P.P.L. at Biggin Hill in a single engine 4 seater Grumman Cheetah.This happened some 20 years after my Fathers' death and I just wish he had lived long enough to see me achieve my flying skill. Unbeknown to him he helped me complete my training. I ran out of money and did not have enough to gain my license. I looked at the shares Dad had left me in Birmid Qualcast, the lawnmower people, and tried to find out if I could earn enough from their sale but could no longer find them listed in the Financial Times. I telephoned my broker who told me that Birmid Qualcast had been bought out by Blue Circle, the cement people, and they had been looking for people who still held their shares. Blue Circle phoned me, I told them how many shares I owned and they offered me 3 for 1. Over night I became what to me was rich. This was enough money to not only finish my training but with a bit left over to buy myself and the family something nice. It was not enough to buy my own

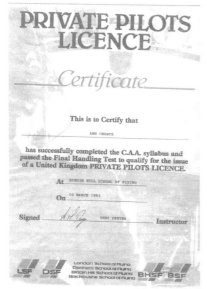

My PPL Licence

Another safe landing with my Grumman Cheetah

aeroplane, but always I thank my Dad for the pleasure and achievement he enabled me to have.

Age was now catching up with me in a few places, throughout my life I had used the services of the NHS for one thing or another some problems were inherited others self inflicted and of course those things that just happen to us naturally.

Both my parents were Migraine sufferers which I inherited from the age of 11. In those days there was no medical help except aspirins. For fellow sufferers, you know that these are no help at all. My Migraines would start without any warnings. Split vision for 20 minutes, pain that has to be endured to understand, vomiting for up to 8 hours, sometimes mild convulsions, and mild paralysis, when tested, no reflexes at all, plus not being able to tell which way was up, therefore very giddy. My Father had a way of trying to help me through the pain. "Always remember my girl, only highly intellectual people get Migraines". It worked for a while but now I know that is not true.

At one point in my life things became so bad that I actually tried to jump out of my bedroom window making it vitally important for my Doctor to visit me and put me out with a Pethadin injection, which very quickly I became addicted to. I finally confessed to this problem and together we managed to wean me off this drug which took 6 weeks of quite hard and determined work.

At the grand age of 36, after two unsuccessful D & C's (Dilate and clean the womb for the uninitiated) I underwent a partial hysterectomy leaving me with my ovaries. On a more serious note I now knew that I could have no more children, which took a while to sink in. I felt that the two very lively spirited ones I had was more than enough to make life worth living. Two years later my tonsils were removed, which I do not recommend that late in life. My Grandmother told me that she got on a tram at Morden,where she lived, went to the Hospital, had her tonsils removed got on a tram and came home. Things have moved forward quite a bit haven't they? On my second day after the tonsillectomy, for my evening meal I was served roast beef, Yorkshire pudding, roast potatoes and cabbage containing a large piece of wire from the strainer which was old and falling to pieces. I complained bitterly and the Matron of the day actually said, "Keep quiet or else everyone will want a piece". After these two major operations I became even more determined to live my life to the full and decided that I would do my best to realise more of my dreams.

I was now at an age when old problems start to re-occur one of them being my knees. In my youth I had been a pairs speed skater, and landing on your knees on the ice doesn't do them a lot of good, mix that with the athletics and gymnastics, I was not surprised to be told that your knees are tired and worn out.

For my 60th Birthday my sons said, "Mum you need some more excitement in your life". They arranged for me to fly a second world war Harvard out of Shoreham and to know that my bottom had been sitting in the same place as a very brave pilot many years previously was very rewarding and moving. Harvards were used during the Second World War to train pilots to land on aircraft carriers. I was not tested out on this type so I had a British Airways pilot at the sharp end and me sitting behind him.

After a short briefing, we were given permission for take off. We were no more than two feet off the ground when the pilot said, "You have a license take over". I yelled, "Take over what?" I had only ever been used to a car steering wheel cut in half as my method of flying, and there wasn't one in this aircraft. The pilot then shouted at me, "There's a big stick waving about somewhere between your legs, GRAB IT". I screamed back, "Where shall we go?" He said, "Preferably up, the runway is rapidly coming to an end". So without further ado I grabbed the controls and lifted off. What a magnificent feeling, to be in the same seat as perhaps one of our brave pilots had been during the war. The pilot told me to fly wherever I wished, as he would do the radio and navigation. For a much larger aircraft than I had ever flown, it was remarkably easier than I had expected it to be. I had been flying for about 15-20 minutes when he grabbed the controls and said, "I have control". I immediately responded with, "You have control".

Without any warning he said, "Do you mind if we do some aerobatics?" Whilst I am saying "Yes" he goes into the first manoeuvre, which consisted of flying upside down, barrel rolls left and right, diving down to the ground and pulling up sharply. Doing this feat meant we were pulling 4g.which as you probably know means that your body now seems to weigh 4 times its actual weight and everything inside you wants to leave and breathing is almost impossible. After 15 minutes of this terrifying activity he is now flying straight and level and heading back to Shoreham.

Getting out of this aircraft is not easy as it is some way off the ground with only one very small foothold to help you. After all this activity in the air I was very giddy and unfortunately fell out of the aircraft into the arms of a very good looking pilot. Things for me always turn out for the best. Before I could do an interview there was only one place I needed to visit in rather an urgent hurry. It was 3 days before I could eat properly again and before the very tight feeling across my forehead disappeared.

At the age of sixty four I decided to learn to ride a horse to enable me to partake in cattle drives across America. To this end I have now done six in total.

In 2005 whilst doing my workout at the local gymnasium I sustained a heart attack. Fortunately for me a lady Doctor was signing in to do her workout and immediately took over. After ten days in Hospital I was allowed to go home to slowly build up my strength again, by changing my food intake, leaving out the butter and walking a little further every day. By now my knees are complaining again, very loudly, so in 2006 I had a total right knee replacement. In 2008 this was swiftly followed by the left knee. I am now the proud possessor of two Titanium knees which set off all the alarm bells at every airport. I am now a bionic Senior Citizen.

I have now for the past nineteen years been a professional after dinner speaker and entertainer. I have two books published by Tucann and in three years have sold 15,000 copies and given back to charities £1,500. I support Air Ambulance, Kent, Surrey, Sussex and Hampshire, Cancer research, Multiple sclerosis and many others too numerous to mention.

Book one relates most of my exploits in my later life and book two is a selection of my odes. Both of which make fun reading but they are not on sale in the shops as too much discount is taken.

From this epistle you can deduce that even after many trials and tribulations I can still get out there and reach for my dreams and my goals. With determination and sheer bloody mindedness I have changed my life completely. So what are you waiting for?

So read on to find out some of my exploits which helped me make the proposed changes.

I hope so. Good Luck.

Chapter Three
"IT'S NOT WHAT YOU KNOW BUT WHO"
Another Of My Dreams Realised.

From the age of eight, another of my dreams was to visit the Grand Canyon.
Having seen photos in my Jesse James album this was a must.

Fortunately my eldest son works for Delta Airlines, therefore, perhaps, the title of this chapter could come true. I started quietly putting suggestions his way, like, "Would you like to take your Mum to America to

21

see one of the great wonders of the world"? It came as a surprise to me that he immediately gave in without a struggle, so my husband and I left him to make all of the necessary plans. On Sunday March 31st 1991 we stayed overnight at his abode and went to the Bricklayers arms for a celebratory evening meal. The last British food we would eat for two weeks. On April fools day we left East Grinstead heading for Gatwick airport. By 10.a.m. we had checked in at the Delta desk and as our son seemed to know everyone of importance we were treated as V.I.P'S. So many of his American colleagues gave us advice on where to go and what to see, we were bogged down with information.

At 11.50.a.m. we boarded a Tristar and were escorted into business class. WOW! So much leg room compared to Economy. (Money talks don't it?) Our coats were taken from us and would you believe hung on a coat hanger in a cupboard and the hand luggage was stowed for us. We were then escorted to the centre of the aircraft next to 1st.Class. Our seats had a reclining leg and back rest, our own individual hide away tables, a T.V. and radio plug, plus all the usual services. At 12.10.a.m the aircraft took off for my first flight to America. Our first drink was free and we were served almonds and cashews on a plate, not in a bag. I felt I could grow to like this life style All our drinks were free and replacements were delivered without having to ask. The stewardesses remembered what each passenger drank, so at no time did you have to remind her/him.

The next treat was an amenity bag which contained a toothbrush, toothpaste, a comb, eye shades and a pair of flight socks. Just to complete the freebies we were given a head set which today you have to pay for.
The piece de resistance was, would you believe, a menu with a choice for lunch of one salad starter, three choices for the main meal, two choices for the desert, plus non-stop coffee and drinks.
After a few hours the Captain came through on the intercom and suggested that if we wished to see Greenland it was visible from the right hand porthole, but please don't all go at once as we might tip sideways. He had a wonderful sense of humour which everyone enjoyed. What a sight Greenland was. My little camera was now working overtime. Then came the in flight movie which was "Sibling Rivalry." in which I was not interested so decided to start my diary.
Some time during the flight I asked the stewardess to ask the Captain, "Where are we"? His reply was lovely. "I think we are in the middle of nowhere but roughly over Newfoundland".Sometime later he announced that for the passengers who really wanted to know our whereabouts, "We are now 100 miles north east of Chimougamoo and hoped that this would clear up the situation for everybody".I already was having a fun time. At 3.00.p.m. local time, we landed in Atlanta where our son collected the next fabulous surprise. A brand new Cadillac Seville, petrol injection, V.8. Engine and fully computerised. When the ignition was switched on it said. "Good Morning", "Good afternoon" or "Good evening". We were told the date, the time, the outside temperature and the inside temperature.
These Yanks have it all don't they?

Our son Ian drove us around Atlanta to see the sights and finally we booked in to the Ramada Inn very hot and exhausted. After a well earned snooze followed by a shower and a complete change of clothing we toddled off to Malones for tea. After this we were all so exhausted we went to bed to recharge the batteries ready for the next days adventures.

Ian in the left hand driving seat, of the Cadillac Seville

The time is now 3.00.a.m and my husband and I are wide awake and raring to go. I think this has something to do with jet lag. As our son was still fast asleep we did our best to keep quiet until 6.00.a.m. This I believe is called youth or an experienced traveller. By 6.45.a.m. luckily we were all awake and after the usual ablutions we went out for my first American breakfast. The menu was confusing, for instance: - Pig in a blanket, ham in a biscuit, sausage in a biscuit or omelette in a biscuit. Whatever happened to good ol'e bacon, egg and fried bread? After this new experience we visited the Lennox shopping mall which is on the north side of Atlanta. WOW! What a size. It was so difficult to comprehend the enormity of this mall that I felt utterly lost in such a vast expanse of shops and diners.

For the next adventure we were driven to my son's boss's ranch in Fayetville Georgia, where we were introduced to all the family including 6 dogs, a goat all the horses and Grand pops. This was a stud ranch for Tennessee trotting stallions and luckily for us it was the mating season.I then witnessed for the first time ever, how horses mate in a stud with a considerable amount of help from the rancher. The rest I will leave to your own vivid imagination. Tennessee trotting stallions are trained from a very young age, where their hooves are gradually built up to twice the normal size to enable them to do what I can only describe as a very high stepping trot. To make them lift their legs higher to allow for the larger feet, large heavy weighted chains plus car tyres are attached to the bridal, and these they have to practice pulling around the training field lifting their legs higher and higher to avoid entanglement with the chains. To me this was not natural and looked very painful and uncomfortable for the poor horses, but the riders were very highly classed in their field of performance which included racing with a two wheel cart or performing what looked like to me some form of dressage. Most of the stallions, like the bosses, chew tobacco and not only do the men spit but so do the horses. We were advised to keep out of the way during spitting sessions.

After many hours of chatting, wondering and drinking home made lemonade our son took us to meet some more of his friends and colleagues. We were made so welcome. The Southern hospitality is something you have to experience to understand. I was always called Miss Ann with that wonderful southern drawl. In the evening we were invited to stay for a barbeque. At one point the husband asked us if we would like to meet his other friends. Being very naïve, we of course said "Yes". We were escorted to his garden shed where we met his pet scorpion and fire ants, both of which are not to be trifled with.

In Georgia all the houses are very South Georgia in style. Very dark interiors, old looking big furniture, lots of frills, four poster beds and a very big ceiling fan in the centre of every room. It gets very hot in South Georgia. After a very long hot and happy day we went back to our hotel for bed.

Roosevelt's Spa.

The next day we were out on the road by 7.30.a.m. and taking of breakfast at Shoney's where you eat as much as you can for $3.89. After food we drove back to the ranch to pick up the wife, also called Miss Ann and her daughter, to visit the warm springs where Roosevelt rehabilitated after polio. Following a barbeque lunch we are off to catch a plane for Phoenix at 7.p.m. See you in Arizona.

Upon arriving in Phoenix we stayed for one night in a Holiday Inn where thanks to our son we obtained quite a good discount. By the next morning we were motoring across the Arizona desert to Flagstaff and then finally on to the Grand Canyon.

As we approached the Canyon my son made me sit on the floor of the car and not open my eyes until I was told to do so. It makes a change when your kids tell you what to do and when. Finally when the car stopped, I was escorted out, still with eyes closed and he walked me to the Canyon rim, whilst gripping his hand very firmly. When he was ready he said, "O.K. Mum you can now open your eyes".I could not believe what I saw. For the first time in my life I was speechless and breathless and spent a lot of time uttering things like ooooh and aaaaah followed by other expletives then finally burst into tears. Even as I write this I can still cry with emotion at the beauty of this wonder of the world. (Excuse me, emotion has caught up again) I had waited for this moment since my 8th Birthday and I could not come to terms with not only where I was but what I was seeing.

My next trip was a surprise, a flight in a twin engine light aircraft for 55 minutes into the Canyon. I was still having a job to cope with my emotions and I was running out of clean and dry hankies.

Looking down from our twin engined light aircraft

After dinner and a very tiring exciting day we all retired early. Our next day was spent travelling around the Canyon and we stayed one night in a Motel. It doesn't matter how many times you visit the Canyon, each time is a different experience. Each day we drove to yet another part of the Canyon and booked into the Yavapai Lodge. The room would not be ready until 4.30.p.m so we took this opportunity to see yet more of this famous Canyon.

After dinner we drove to the rim to take photos of the famous sunset. This has to be seen to be believed. The changes in colour are rapid and

25

AWESOME as the Americans say. Many photographers stay there all night just to get the first picture of sunrise. We British like our beds more than the sunrise, so that's where we all went.

The next morning we left the Lodge and drove along the Eastern rim to the desert view point followed by our visit to Bryce Canyon some 285 miles away. En route we drove through the Painted Desert and the Navajo Indian reservation where we encountered a number of stalls selling Indian hand made jewellery. As you can imagine I was hooked and purchased some of their wares. Finally at 5.00.p.m. we arrived in Bryce Canyon and booked into a Motel at the fantastic price of $39 per night. After going to the Canyon on the advice of the Motel staff to see yet another fabulous sunset we went to a saloon for dinner. As the clocks are to go forward 1 hour tonight due to time change zone we are going to have an early night. ZZZZZZZZZZZZZZZZZZZ.

After a good night's kip and a hearty breakfast we all felt ready for Bryce Canyon. It is just my personal opinion but this Canyon is almost more spectacular than the Grand Canyon. The different colours of rusty red/brown and the snow makes it a wonderland of maces, buttes and hoodoos. I'm only showing off my cowboy lingo here. I don't know what all these names mean, but it makes me sound extremely smart. My son and I descended into the canyon and we walked the Navajo loop trail covered in snow, ice and mud. A truly wonderful trip. This walk was described as moderate to strenuous, which in my opinion was a gross understatement. Having walked and slipped through thick ice and snow, on arriving at the bottom of the canyon it was so hot we did not know what to do with ourselves apart from melt.

You have to see this scenery to believe it.

Having found my Husband who was not able to do the walk we rested and had lunch in yet another diner. Once again fully refreshed we drove to the Petrified Forest in Escalante where there is a fabulous nature trail taking you up the mountain. We struggled for at least 1 and a half hours in extreme heat and very strong winds, but what we saw made the effort worthwhile. We came across a petrified juniper tree, lichen and many organisms. In the distance we could see deer and some wolves. There were enormous black boulders that had been ejected from volcanoes many years ago. It was like stepping back into the past

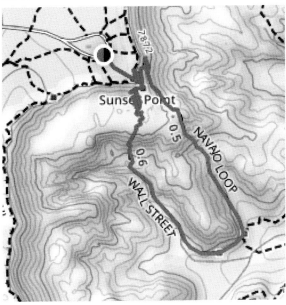

The area was covered in petrified

Spectacular scenery on the Navajo loop

trees, so old they were now solid rock. Absolutely fascinating. The final touch was that we saw no other human beings all day. If you go into the countryside it's never crowded, only with animals, flora and fauna. Our next port of call was an enormous reservoir and an R.V. park. If you care to write

27

in and ask me I will tell you what R.V. stands for. Later on the same day we went into Escalante which is a typical desert Mormon town. Although Mormons make up a large part of the population we also saw Amish families

An Amish buggy tied up out side a grocery store.

who are all dressed in black and drive buggies not cars. This is a complete eye opener as to how some people can live happily without the use of modern equipment.

The next day we are off to Las Vegas to see how much we can afford to lose on the gaming tables. Our journey took us through Zion Park where you pay $10 to drive through an enormous hole cut into the mountain. It was the best $10 worth I have ever spent. Zion Park is volcanic and the mountains are chocolate in colour, so to make the scenery more spectacular the road has been paved the same colour as the mountains. This route, pronounced rowte if you are American, was very steep and winding, a little bit nerve racking, but so beautiful. Our son coped very well as all youngsters do. We stopped in a small town called Mesquite for lunch, (as you do) visited a Casino and unfortunately we lost some more dollars.

As we were now driving through yet another time zone we gained an hour and arrived in Las Vegas one hour before we left our last port of call. The Las Vegas Hilton was our bed for the night at a cost of just $60. In the evening we have booked to see "The Best Show in Town", with 100 girls depicting the sinking of the Titanic. There appeared to be only young slim naked girls on the ship who danced and wriggled in a massive swimming pool on the stage. In our opinion it couldn't have been further from reality, but that's America for you. The males in the audience loved it, and so did our son. Ian, suggested that we tip the steward $5 to get a private booth with a great view. Beer was

$4 a glass but the water was free, so after a while we developed a taste for, yes, you've guessed it Water. The show was fabulous and cost $30,000,000 to produce. We paid a mere $38.10 for the three of us, plus the tip and a few beers. Not bad eh?

The next day at 7.45.a.m. we said a fond farewell to Las Vegas. Somewhere en route, oops rowte, we all partook of a great breakfast at Harry's café in downtown Boulder city Nevada. I'm slowly getting the hang of the language of the West. Harry's was a 50's diner which had an old time soda fountain,something I used to see in the old American movies. For me, the next piece of excitement was to drive across the Hoover Dam, which is Dam big. Then across the Mohave Desert which is very hot, dusty and full of enormous Sequoya cactus, snakes, vultures and scorpions. Along the way there were many signs telling tourists not to stray into the desert as the risk of being bitten by a snake or a scorpion was very high. As we were good British tourists we did as suggested and surveyed the scene from a distance.

The airport at Phoenix was our next stop where we were to take a flight to Atlanta. Unfortunately there were no standby seats available so we were not downhearted as our son arranged for us to fly to Los Angeles where we could at last get a flight back to Atlanta. If not for our son being an employee of Delta airlines I think there is a good chance we might still be waiting at the airport for a flight home to England. On arrival in Atlanta we hired a Chrysler New Yorker and drove out to the Gage Ranch in Fayetville Georgia where we stayed as guests for one night. In the evening the Gage family took us out for dinner to a local diner, where we had to speak very loudly to allow everyone to hear our, to them, posh English accent. We tried to copy their accents and they tried to copy ours. The owner of the diner said that he had never had so much fun during dinner time. We spent the entire evening just eating and communicating with our friends and all the locals who by now were also our good friends. Well this was the South.

Breakfast the next day was at Shoney's where you can eat as much as you like for $5. Both the men in my family made good use of this privilege. During the day we lazed in the sunshine on the Ranch, doing as little as possible. One of the Gage's daughters happened to be a hairdresser so the two men decided to have a hair cut, for nothing, again, not what you know but who. During the day the owner of the ranch gave me the privilege to ride a full blown Tennessee Trotting Stallion walker called Goldie. He was so big and powerful but so well trained I experienced no problems. Lunch was served at the Lone Star. WOW! What food. We all felt we would miss this life style back home in England. It's now our last night in Georgia and we were once again taken out to dinner, where we were entertained by an Elvis Presley look alike. He was quite good and fun to watch. This for me was true country and western style at its best. Sadly we are now on our way to Atlanta airport to resume normal living in England. It's a shame but,

WE'RE ALL GONNA COME BACK SOON NOW, YA HEAR?
There's another dream under my belt.
I'm still working on not only making my life a bit better, but for others at the same time.

Chapter Four

WATCH OUT AMERICA.........
HERE WE COME AGAIN.
September 5th to 20th 2002.

This is yet another adventure where I took my disabled client Valerie to see the wild and woolly west of America. For me it had been a quiet year so once again I was looking for ways to realise more dreams. After the usual long hours of organising this trip, plus many visits to the local shopping mall for suitable summer clothing, we both felt ready for anything that might happen. (Some people are naïve ain't they?) A local taxi firm, which catered for wheelchair access collected us both at 9.20 am to deliver us to the North Terminal of Gatwick Airport. On arrival, help came very quickly after our driver had telephoned for wheelchair assistance. At the check in desk we went through first with no waiting. You see if you travel with a friend in a wheelchair, you get preferential treatment. Much to Valerie's excitement we were subjected to no less than two body searches plus a wheelchair search. With no drugs found hidden under Valerie's posterior, or in the tubing of the wheelchair, she was cleared. The entire luggage went through the radar and we were both pronounced ALL CLEAR. Then we experienced the first little glitch. We had to wait in the departure lounge for over an hour as the plane was late due to fog, and the aircraft was suffering hydraulics malfunction. At this point I wanted to scream for my eldest son who at the time was the chief maintenance manager at Gatwick for Delta airlines. We were flying British Airways, but I knew my son's capabilities and wished that he could help. Finally when the problem was sorted we were escorted on to a Boeing 777 to discover that someone was in our seats, which I had previously booked well in advance due to Valerie's disability. A young mother with a small child had preference over someone with a physical disability, that's why she was given our seat. After a bit of slightly heated complaining by my good self plus a lot of people movement we were finally found alternative seating. I was informed that we could not sit next to the bulkhead as arranged, due to the fact that the arm rest did not lift up making exit for a disabled person difficult. Would you believe we were put one row behind, which strangely had the same problem, so all my hard work in booking seats in advance was wasted .The cabin crew seemed to have no knowledge of the workings of the aircraft they were flying in. This is a very comforting thought isn't it? With this entire ruckus taking place we had now delayed the departure time even further, much to the annoyance of the rest of the passengers. We finally became airborne at 2.00.p.m (7.30.a.m. Denver time) for a 9 hour 25 minute flight. Lunch was not served until 3.45.p.m. and nothing had passed our lips for over 8 hours. When the stewardess arrived she said, "Do you want Chicken Tika or Salmon?"We both ordered the Salmon to be told, "Sorry it's all gone". Valerie decided to have the chicken and after a very long wait they found me a Salmon. Can you catch fish over the pond at 35,000 feet? The coffee was served but also unfortunately not only did they run out of cups but they ran out of coffee as well. What a fabulous advert for British Airways, but lets' think positive as we are now comfortably cruising at 35,000 feet over an ice flow. WOW what a sight! Fortunately for us, nothing else untoward happened for a few hours, but soon this would change. Valerie needed to answer a call of nature. The toilet doorway, as most of you are aware is only wide enough to get in, if you turn your body sideways. This does not accommodate wheelchair access. A stewardess called Sascha, told us that, "Normally, all disabled passengers are fitted with colostomies or catheters". "Our staff is not used to dealing with people who have normal bodily functions but can't use their legs". I am not permitted to put in writing my reply, suffice it to say I was a LITTLE BIT CROSS and that was the nearest I have ever been to giving someone a right uppercut. So, let's move on and try to be positive.

We arrived in Denver at about 3.30.p.m. (local time 11.00.p.m.) and as you can imagine, both feeling a bit weary and wondering what else could befall us. On being helped to disembark we were greeted by a group of very tall, very black men, who were the best thing that had happened to us for hours. They were not only so helpful but made us laugh and kept us amused. After finding and identifying our luggage this was put on the onward flight to Jackson Hole. Another very helpful girl arrived to take us to the departure lounge. Next problem................ Our tickets did not state which concourse to go to, so after 2 trains, a 1 mile walk, and 30 minutes later we arrived at our destination gate for departure. I was now very tired. Have you ever pushed a wheelchair one mile through a crowded concourse, not knowing exactly where to go? We finally arrived at the announced gate number which after 5 minutes was changed yet again. Unfortunately, due to the noise level, we never heard this announcement and nearly missed the flight. This was not our day. But, are we downhearted? Yes we certainly are at the moment. I said to myself, "Come on Ann you can cope with this little technical problem or at least pretend you can for the sake of Valerie".This was still not going to be our day. As we boarded the small plane to Jackson, our allocated seats had again been changed from 3D and 3E first class to 17A and 17B tourist class. The plane was half- empty so although I objected very strongly I didn't win. I thought why does no one like us? What have I done to upset America? Again, the armrests would not rise and there was no one available to help me get Valerie into her seat. To physically lift a disabled person over an arm rest in a very small plane is definitely not recommended even for a tough guy. This is service or so it says in the brochure. My local tour operator said she had informed all the airlines we were using, that help at every turn was needed, but it must have been ignored. Finally, taking pity on the two us, one passenger and the steward finally offered to help me get Valerie seated in this very old dilapidated aircraft. Can you truly understand the humiliation that a disabled person sometimes has to put up with?

The weather was deteriorating rather rapidly, but being truly British we adopted the stiff upper lip and put our faith and trust in the pilots. Throughout this two and a half hour flight we flew through a very bad storm and were struck by lightning. The sight was spectacular to see the sky lit up like bonfire night. But.........if I'm honest we were both rather frightened. One hour later after flying through the storm we landed safely at Jackson Hole airport. Once again the dye was cast. Nobody was available or strong enough to help me lift Valerie over the fixed armrests. But with a lot of blood, sweat, tears and swearing, this feat was finally achieved. The time is now 9.30.p.m. and the airport is dark and deserted as everyone else has knocked off for the day. I started to frantically look for the off loaded wheelchair, which, without any airport staff help I located it under the nose wheel of the aircraft we had just landed in. Alone and without assistance I lifted Valerie from the airport wheelchair into her own and made our way to the Avis car hire desk to pick up our Silver Grey Buick.

Valerie, happy to be on land after arriving at Jackson Hole airport.

Guess what, the counter is empty and no one to help me yet again. I literally went behind the counter into their office to tell them that I had pre- booked a car and needed someone to give me a key and sign the paperwork, After some slight disagreement, paperwork was completed and I was given the key. "Nearly sorted", I said to Valerie, "leave it to me I will not be beaten". With key in one hand, pushing the wheelchair with the other I manoeuvred the trolley containing our suitcases with my THIRD hand. The next task was to locate the vehicle which was somewhere parked in this enormous, very dark car park, where again not a soul in sight to even offer some assistance. Eventually on finding the said car I loaded the suitcases, moved Valerie from her wheelchair to the front seat, put the wheel chair in the enormous trunk as they say in US of A and settled into the driving seat of this very large unfamiliar Buick. After 5 minutes I discovered where to put the ignition key, switched on and the engine roared into life. To my horror this car had no hand brake that I could find, so what to do now? I left Valerie alone in the car whilst I went looking for advice. Sometimes the real things that happen are what make a good story. I found a cleaner who felt sorry for me and she came out to the car park to show me how to drive this car. Truth of the matter is that it did not have a hand brake. When the car is put into neutral the brake goes on automatically. Why didn't I think of that? I now felt a little more confident, revved the engine, located my local map, chose forward gear and slowly began to move to try to find the exit. I am now in a strange automatic large Buick, in my opinion on the wrong side of the road, driving in a very mountainous area, no street lights, late at night, local time just after midnight. I tried very hard to find the Best Western Lodge in Teton village. I could swear that it had been moved without my knowledge. There are not a lot of people milling about at that time of the morning, perhaps a few inebriates, but they didn't know where they were let alone tell me where I was. After what seemed an eternity I finally located our first stop. With an enormous sigh of relief, I left Valerie in the car as I went to book in. This Hotel had been booked and paid for in England some 6 months prior so, I was not expecting what happened next. I smiled pleasantly on approaching the male receptionist, who in a few rude and unpleasant words said," You can't stay here because Dick Cheney has taken over the entire Hotel for a Security Conference".Modesty once again does not permit me to tell you exactly what my response was. Can you imagine how we both felt, after 2 separate flights from England some 15 hours ago, experiencing some technical difficulties at both Gatwick and Jackson Hole airports, we had not eaten or drunk for over 7 hours and Valerie was in desperate need of the toilet. How will I deal with this situation? I argued vehemently without success, and if I am being honest for once in my life, I had a few tears of temper and frustration at being treated so badly. The off hand attitude of the desk clerk even made things more unbearable. In a calmer moment I told them about Valerie outside in her wheelchair, unable to walk and requested that they let me bring her in just to make use of the toilet facilities as this for her was now so urgent. Their answer goes down in American history. They declined saying, "The American Security Staff are in charge". I tried

33

pleading, reasoning and down right rudeness but nothing would shift them. Perhaps disabled people in America don't have the same needs as us Brits. What a thoughtless and unfeeling bunch of people I had to deal with. The time now is 11.00.p.m. local time 4.00a.m. GMT. I am now known as DESPERATE Ann with a toilet ban. After much more wrangling with the unhelpful clerk, he made a phone call and booked us into the Snow King Hotel in the mountainous region of Jackson Hole. I told him that I would need directions and begrudgingly he scribbled some notes on a bit of paper. We set off again but Valerie is now almost in tears as her need is urgent and so is mine. I am now very tired, driving in the pitch dark through the mountainous region with hairpin bends that nearly made me wet my pants. After some time the Hotel did not appear where it should have done. I had no choice, the only place I knew was the Best Western, and I retraced my steps to ask for further help. I was told in no uncertain terms by MY FRIEND at the desk, that most people can find the Hotel, it's easy, just follow my instructions. It's now 11.30.p.m. local time but according to our stomachs it must be nearer to breakfast time. What shall I do now, I asked myself? Again, I'm ashamed to admit it; I lost my temper and had a few exasperated tears. I can cope with this problem and if necessary I can go anywhere to answer my call of nature but not so for my disabled friend. Just as I thought my world was about to come to an end, a lady truck driver sitting in the foyer said, "Follow me in my truck I will take you there, it's not easy to find, even for us locals". I glared at the receptionist and was longing to say something detrimental to his health, but I declined. Oh, Wow, you see there is light at the end of the tunnel and somebody does care, I thought, but then, you know what thought did, he only thought he did.

With great relief and much thanking of the truck driver we finally arrived at this new Hotel. I wearily approached the receptionist, announced who I was and waited for a suitable reply. In the words of John Denver "Some days are diamonds, some days are stones". Today was one of those days, STONES. The previous Hotel had only booked a room for one person and only one night. According to GMT it was now 4.00.a.m and I am in no mood to be told this information. I am now almost out of control in the bad words and temper department and unfortunately it was the receptionist who got the rough edge of my tongue. She was very polite and helpful and the matter was finally rectified, but I had to sleep on a camp bed. I was now so very tired that everything I had to do to help Valerie into the toilet, get undressed and into bed was almost more than I could manage. Fatigue does very strange things to your body. It's as if you are not quite on this planet and sleep seems to be impossible, even though that is all you really want to do. If this is the way we were to be treated by some very unkind Americans, we were not looking forward to the rest of the two weeks. How could the situation get any worse? I bet you can make an educated guess at this moment in time can't you?

The next morning by 6.45.a.m we were both awake and trying to think in a positive frame of mind. So after ablutions we made our way to the dining room for breakfast. This was the first food and drink we had had for

34

over 15 hours. By now we were both so exhausted we did nothing all day. The weather was appalling. It was raining sideways, blowing a very strong wind and the visibility was ZERO. Apart from that everything was looking fine. Oh no it wasn't!! Our toilet has now become blocked and I thought this only happened in hot poorer countries. So I called the desk for help. Luckily after only a very short time a maintenance man knocked on our door. He turned out to be a young ex naval man from Texas. After the toilet had been repaired we spent a very happy half hour just chatting with this charming man. The entire day has now nearly gone and we are too exhausted to do anything. It's still raining cats and dogs, with torrents of water cascading down the slope outside the Hotel. We were told that there is a serious threat of floods and gales. GOSH! I bet you're glad you're not here with us in America. We both paid over £1,000 each to experience the same weather we get regularly in England. We are now both peed off, very tired, a bit bored and we are still not sure if we are hungry. But after supper, before retiring, we decided to plan the next day's adventure. This was to leave Jackson Hole after breakfast, Yipee! Drive through the Teton Mountains to try to find Yellowstone Park in the rain, floods, mist and low cloud. Oh Boy! What an adventure we are having and its only day three. In the morning we awoke quite early, did what women need to do to make you look better than the night before, ate our first hearty breakfast and packed our bags ready for the next part of the journey. As I handed back the room key to the receptionist, she gave me the bill. I discovered that she had charged my debit card for the two nights accommodation, even though she had promised me that this would not happen. As we had already paid the other Hotel, I politely pointed out that they were not going to get my money twice and suggested that the Snow King Hotel get the money they were owed from the delinquent Hotel. I now made my feelings felt very vehemently and refused to leave until my debit card had been credited with the correct amount. Finally satisfied, I thanked the Manageress for her help and we happily left the Snow King behind us without any fond memories so far.

The weather seemed to be improving so with a happy heart we drove off to find the Old Faithful Inn in Yellowstone Park. At around lunchtime we pulled into a lay-by and ate a hearty snack. As we ate we watched the intermittent rain and listened to many loud claps of thunder. Quite exciting we thought.

After our break we took a scenic drive through the parks ravaged by fires, think how little influence we, as human beings have, over Mother Nature. What a devastating sight. After quite a long drive we finally found the Old Faithful Inn with the famous geyser of the same name. We couldn't have timed it better; she was just about to blow as she does roughly every 90 minutes. How could we check in just yet? The most important thing to do was to grab our cameras and record this momentous occasion. What a sight. Nature is wonderful

After this bit of unexpected excitement we checked into the Old Faithful Inn. This has to be seen to fully understand exactly what it looks like. It's very old looking with a very dark entrance hall and completely

The Teton Mountains

Inside reception area of the Old Faithfull Inn

made of wood. Just like the cabins you might see in the old cowboy movies. Enormous long round logs both inside and outside made up the solid structure. This was realising another of my dreams, to live in a log cabin. Mind you this one was enormous, oh, but what the hell, a girl can dream. In the centre of the lobby a big log fire burnt making you feel very warm and welcome. The next amazing sight was hanging from the very tall ceiling which must have been at least 25 feet high, an enormous clock pendulum gently swinging whilst the clock ticked quietly and methodically. It reminded me of Edgar Alan Poe's story of the Pit and the Pendulum. The lobby was overlooked by balconies on three sides complete with easy chairs to enable visitors to sit and watch the world go by.

After settling into our room, we felt that we should go and eat dinner, but we found ourselves exhausted, suffering from jet lag and altitude. We are at 8,500 feet in a very dry atmosphere, something we were both not used to yet. We made a big decision; fell into bed at 9.30.p.m. very dirty and very tired. Never mind we thought, things will now improve and tomorrow is another day.

The next day, which was Sunday, we slept in for a while, until hunger got the better of us. So after our ablutions we made our way to the restaurant and had a rather large breakfast to make up for having no dinner the previous night. Now feeling much stronger and more refreshed and raring to go, I pushed Valerie in her wheelchair on the boardwalks around several amazing geysers all blowing away merrily. We saw deep holes in the ground containing beautiful blue water which was boiling and bubbling and occasionally erupting into the air. Throughout the Yellowstone Park there are numerous fumaroles spitting sulphur and other minerals, covering the ground in a mixture of colours mostly yellow. Perhaps this is why it is called Yellowstone. You see, some of us are very smart. Just as we walked by Old Faithful, it blew its top yet again.

We then decided to have lunch in our room, where we met the cleaner who was a young Polish student. (A good looking male).Throughout our lunch break we were watched through our bedroom window by a very large Bison. When you are that close to this animal you immediately realise how large and intimidating they are. After a short rest to let the lunch go down I drove the car further into the park to see enormous calderas, lakes, rivers, fumaroles, beehive geysers, boiling steam and water and a rather large herd of Bison. Being rather larger than us we gave them a wide berth. I then decided to take the car up a very narrow road to Fire Creek where we encountered a very large Elk blocking our path. Not only did we see hundreds more Bison but two very small chipmunks. This car ride lasted for nearly two and a half hours through wonderful scenery. On arriving back at The Old Faithful Inn, we decided to eat at the Snow Lodge and then, when we felt well fed and happy we at last fell into bed. Today, Monday, we are off to Billings. So after breakfast we left Yellowstone and the Old Faithful Inn and immediately ran into another very large herd of Bison walking leisurely through the car park. Trust me, you do not argue with Bison, so we had to wait patiently whilst they finally got out of the way.

I even had time to get some close up shots of these magnificent animals, even one of them looking through my driver's side window. SCARY. Free at last I then drove to places with wonderful names for example, West Thumb, Bridge Bay, Sulphur Cauldron, the Grand Canyon of Yellowstone, finally driving the car over Bear Tooth pass at 13,000feet. COR!!!I never realised that I could drive a car round so many "S" bends and still remain on the road. I thought my sons would be proud of my skill and daring do. It's now just another 177 miles to Billings. We drove through Cody, Powell, the Shoshone National Forest and Mammoth Springs. These town names sound a lot more interesting than Balham or Tooting. Each small town that we drove through tells you the name and the population. The smallest town contained only 5 residents. After a bit of a struggle we finally located our Hotel, The Sheraton. The room was O.K. but it was situated in a large railway siding. All night long we could hear the freight trains sounding their horns. I did not "Long to hear the train whistle blow". Their noise is very reminiscent of U.S.A, but stops anyone getting any sleep. I really feel that these two weeks will be memorable if nothing else. Billings is a very small town with nothing to do or see, so we went for a short car ride. Lucky for us, we found two shops open and both selling what we felt was rubbish. We knew we would be rather glad to leave Billings. So, with a happy heart we departed in the morning to drive to Buffalo, a one hos' town where our next accommodation was situated. Surprise, surprise, our room is in a large lorry car park, where our bedroom window faced all the large vehicles which came and went throughout the long night. Almost as exciting as Billings!!!! Not much to do here either, but I did find a very old small museum where after 5 minutes we had seen it all. The town also had a Bank, where I changed some money. That was Billings.

Do you remember I said that things could not get worse? There are times when you wish you had kept your mouth shut. I now don't feel well;

I have a very bad sore throat and a high temperature, but for Valerie's sake I must keep a stiff upper lip. With mixed feelings we left Billings for Rapid City, via Gillette. On our way we stopped off at the Devils Tower, Buffalo Bill Country, in Wyoming. This towering ancient rock overlooks the Belle Fourche River. I have tried to translate this from the French and all I can come up with is,"Beautiful Forked River". The tower is visible for miles, probably because of the height. It would be impossible to say that you couldn't find it. This rock is 1,000 feet across the bottom and 275 feet across the top. It rises 1,280 feet above the valley to a height of 5,117 feet above sea level. Legend has it that it was worshipped by the local Indians and is believed to be an old volcanic plug. Devils Tower became a National Monument on September 24th 1906.

The Devil's Tower.

After leaving the Devils Tower we motored on through the Black Hills National Forest in Dakota, which originally was owned by the Sioux Indian. Then we drove through a town called Spearfish. I have to admit at this point that I became slightly unaware of my geographical location. In other words, I got lost, but finally made it to Deadwood which came rolling over the Black Hills of Dakota. These hills are so called not due to the colouration of the soil or rock, but due to the thick ponderosa pine forests, which from a distance appears black. Valerie and I could not resist singing very loudly the song made famous by Doris Day. "Take me back to the Black Hills the Black Hills of Dakota". I don't think we would ever have been offered a singing part in any musical. Sometime after lunch we finally arrived in Rapid City South Dakota, otherwise known as the Windy City. Oh boy is it, but also very hot and dry. There's another song here. I'll leave a blank space here for the reader to give their own version.

All finished? Did you do well? Wait for it, there are more problems looming. On checking in at our pre-booked Holiday Inn, we were rather bluntly informed that there were no rooms available with wheelchair accessibility. I explained that this had been paid for and booked 6 months ago by our tour operator in England who had also telephoned to confirm same. We were told that the couple who were supposed to vacate our room had decided to stay on a few extra days. The Hotel had agreed and we were left with a room with no disability facilities. I complained as hard as I knew how but to no avail. We stayed here for one night trying very hard to cope. I manage as I can walk, but poor Valerie was in trouble yet again. The toilet door in our room was not wide enough to allow access to a wheelchair. My only option was to go to the 3rd floor where there was a toilet for the disabled to allow Valerie to answer a call of nature. In the middle of the night I can assure you this is not fun. There next followed a bit more "Excitement".Security men had taken over the 3rd floor and we were told in no uncertain terms that "we could not use this floor". You can probably guess my response, but roughly translated I told the men that as every living creature needed to answer a call of nature, no large imposing armed men would stop me taking my friend to do what they could do where and whenever they needed to.

This bit is great. Every time I needed to escort Valerie to the loo, the security guard waited outside the lavatory door and after we vacated they actually went in and searched the toilet to make sure we had not planted anything suspicious. I was very tempted to do something naughty at this point but Valerie put her foot down with a firm hand and forbade me to do what was on my mind. The next day we were given a different room, but still with only one proper bed, mine was a fold up job. The Hotel tried to make amends by giving us a free meal. It didn't solve the problem but we both felt that perhaps they had some understanding of the problems they had caused. So with a slightly happier heart, determination and a full breakfast inside us we drove to Mount Rushmore to view these strange phenomena of famous busts of past American politicians carved into a hillside. The entrance fee in our opinion was far too expensive for what we were to see. To reach the cliff face I had to push the wheelchair up an enormous hill. No facilities were on hand to help people like myself. I was rather glad when we had seen the faces and could make our way down the hill somewhat quicker than my ascent. We both felt that this had been a bit of a con but an experience to be remembered. After leaving Mount Rushmore I drove to a small town called Keystone, which had a mined out gold mine. So… were we downhearted …Oh no! I bought two tickets for the visit and after we were both issued with hard hats I pushed Valerie in her wheelchair 600 feet into the gold mine. It was better for my friend as the ceiling was very low, but not good for me as I had to bend double whilst pushing her chair.

Mount Rushmore.
Carvings from L to R
George Washington,
Thomas Jefferson
Theodore Roosevelt
Abraham Lincoln

'Big Thunder' an old
empty gold mine

The temperature in the mine was quite cold but a wonderful adventure for Valerie. Unfortunately there was no gold left so we are both as poor now as we were when we left England.

Unfortunately for me the throat problem is getting worse and my temperature is now quite high. I enquired at our Hotel if there was a surgery near by. The answer was, "Yes, it's just across the road". The most dangerous part of this visit was trying to cross a 6 lane highway but I finally managed it and arrived at the surgery in one piece. I was diagnosed with a bronchial infection. The fee was $84 plus $19 for the prescription. I'm now not only feeling poorly but poor as well.

After leaving the windy city we took a very long scenic drive through towns called Black Hill, Hot Springs and Chadron en route to Douglas. When lunch was over it was back to the car for more scenic driving through Nebraska National Forest, Pine Ridge National Forest and finally arriving in Douglas for an overnight stop. In the morning after a well earned rest and recuperation, the plan was to drive to Cheyenne. Some plans don't always pan out do they? On searching a map of the area, one thing sprang to my attention; we could make a detour and visit the famous Fort Fetterman. Fort Fetterman was built in 1867 by the United States Army, situated on the bluff of the North Platte River near the original Bozeman trail on the Great Plains frontier in the Dakota Territory. Being a keen follower of the White man versus the Red man history, this visit was a must. With great excitement I

41

searched my map, located the Fort and with uncontrollable feelings drove into the grounds of the Fort. You can almost guess what comes next. It was closed for the season. So: not to be outdone, I pushed Valerie in her wheelchair where many a Native Indian and U.S. Cavalry had trod. This did something to make me feel the emotion inside me. Fortunately we were completely alone in a very deserted Fort Fetterman, with not an army man or Indian in sight. Having seen all we could in the Fort we drove on again over the River Platte to a place called Guernsey National Forest. This is a very beautiful enormous park with a small entrance fee of $10. Due to the fact that this time of the year was close season for most American tourists, we were again completely alone in this wonderland. At no time did we feel nervous or threatened by any animals. Throughout the park we saw a brand new dam and reservoir and some of the most scenic canyons and rivers. Fortunately, with hindsight, I had packed a picnic for this days touring. This was a good choice as all the facilities in the park were closed. After a while spent searching for a suitable place to eat, we came across a fabulous picnic area, and did what all tourists do, we ate our picnic.
The beauty and tranquillity of this area was superb. We are all inclined to believe that the U.S.A is so crowded and full of traffic, but, if you get off the beaten track life can be sweet. We are the only folk around for miles. This is the way to enjoy the countryside, the rivers, birds, flora and fauna. There was only one small problem; the toilets in the picnic area were prehistoric, or to be more polite, needed some modernisation!!!!! The next twenty minutes or so I will leave to your vivid imagination. Finally we left Guernsey and drove to Fort Laramie, where the MAN came from. This was another important sight for me to see. Fort Laramie was built by the fur traders in 1834. By 1849 the U.S. Military bought the Fort, which is now a National Monument.
In March of 1870 Laramie witnessed the first ever woman to serve on a jury. In 1871 another first: Laramie saw the first woman ever to vote in a general election. Although neither of us saw "The man from Laramie", visiting this Fort was like stepping back in time again and trying to imagine how the cavalry lived in days of yore. After Laramie we went to see the original deep ruts still very visible which were left by the Oregon Trail Pioneers. There is so much history in this part of America and we both felt very privileged to visit these historic sights. Following on from all this excitement we are now back in the car driving through very small hick towns one of which was called Torrington. Luckily for us we have now at last found Cheyenne. Someone up there is not very fond of me. The Hotel booking was again incorrect. One room was booked for us, but only a roller bed once again for me, resulting in very little manoeuvrability for the wheelchair in our room. But as you can imagine, being truly British and full of grit, we made the best of a bad job. I am confident that all travellers reading this problem will share my annoyance. When we arrive home in England the tour operator will very soon know how disgruntled we both were.
After two days in Cheyenne we packed our bags and left this city behind us and motored on to Denver, driving through the Estees National Park

42

and the Big Thompson River and Dam. Well, not literally through the river, or over the Dam, but very near.

With a bit of a struggle in Downtown Denver we finally located the 4 points Cherry Creek Sheraton Hotel. I bet you can guess what happened next. Only a room again booked with one bed and that being in Valerie's name, therefore they could not confirm the booking. A frantic phone call was made to England to our tour operator and after some fairly heated exchanges the Hotel, upon realising their mistake, politely grovelled and accepted our booking. We thought, now we can relax for a while and enjoy Denver. I am now very sure that someone doesn't want us to have a good time. Our room has no facilities for wheelchair access and only one bed. Where do they think I am going to sleep? I hot footed back down to reception and as politely as I could I complained and suggested that if they could only read the information on my booking form they would very quickly learn what was needed. Finally we were escorted to another room with at least a toilet for the disabled, but once more, only one bed. So once again I camped on a roller bed squashed in a corner of the room. It was quite laughable to see me climbing over my bed to help Valerie out of bed each morning. As I know, laughter is one way of overcoming adversity. The Hotel did their best to say sorry, by giving us two free breakfasts and a very genuine apology. This was at least some improvement. After an evening meal, I have to be honest we were both a bit fed up so decided to lie in bed and watch the many T.V. channels. Too many to choose from, so we switched off and settled down for the night.

The next day dawned and with a new vigour, suitably showered and well fed we planned what to do. I had arranged to meet an acquaintance at the Hotel, but for the second time he cancelled the visit. He is no longer on my list of friends. The good news was that we now could have the whole day to ourselves and do whatever we pleased. With a spring in my step and the wheelchair suitably oiled and polished we went for a long walk in the park, where as luck would have it we found an ice cream stall. Yes you've guessed it; we both made a pig of ourselves and ate one of the biggest ice creams I have ever seen. My excuse was that I had to push the wheelchair for over two miles before reaching our Hotel. A growing "Girl" needs sustenance to keep up her strength. But that was not all, it suddenly started to rain very hard and we had taken no waterproofs with us. I covered Valerie's lap with plastic bags which rapidly filled with water. We finally arrived back at the Hotel looking like two drowned rats, but happily laughing. The river running alongside the Hotel was in fear of flooding so a bit more excitement ensued. Luckily the torrential downpour ceased, out came the sun and life began to return to some sort of normality.

After drying out and partaking of lunch we decided to order a Yellow Taxi cab to take us to Downtown Denver. This was not quite what we had hoped for. In our opinion, the shops were not very tempting; the streets were very noisy and crowded. We'd seen enough and wanted to go back to our Hotel. I needed help to call for a taxi, so I put on this British, "please help a poor English women with a friend in a wheelchair and phone for a taxi".

It worked and after some twenty minutes the taxi found us outside the shop that had been very helpful and transported us back to the Sheraton Hotel. Guess what? More mistakes. This time it was my fault. To get the wheelchair into the taxi I had to remove the footplates. These I left on the sidewalk (that's pavement, just in case you didn't know) somewhere in Downtown Denver. The taxi driver took me back again to see if they were where I had left them, but I was not so lucky, someone had lifted them. Who on earth would want or need two National Health Service wheelchair footplates? But there you go; Valerie could get a new set when we arrived home in England. Two footplates have now been donated to posterity, courtesy of the N.H.S.

After a rest I took Valerie to the Cherry Creek shopping Mall. It doesn't matter how many times I visit one of these enormous Malls I still get lost and a bit confused. We didn't buy a thing, just looked. We're not very good for business are we? The next day we start our journey back to England. In the morning after breakfast we left the Hotel for Denver airport.

You would think that anyone can find such a large location. Unfortunately I am not anyone. It took some time to locate, and I even went onto the wrong side of the road once, as I forgot in my panic, that I was in America. They drive on the opposite side of the road to us in England!!! No police were visible so I got away with this little digression. Now I have admitted it in print perhaps I could get arrested. With my skill and perspicacity, whatever that means, the airport came into view and I drove the hire car to the well signed returning point and settled any outstanding monies. Once they realised that Valerie was in a wheelchair they drove us to the airport. The courtesy they showed us was wonderful and our thoughts about America began to change a little. At the airport we checked in our luggage, booked our seats on the aircraft and patiently waited for the announcement to board the plane. On boarding, we were told in no uncertain terms by the stewards, "We are not paid or qualified to put disabled people onto a plane or help them visit the toilet". On asking for help to get Valerie to the toilet the steward said, "Most disabled people have a catheter fitted, so why hasn't your friend got one"? After that remark, it was the second time I have ever been so near to decking someone. After some POLITE argument my request was dealt with.

Some 7 and a half hours later we arrived in England, very glad to be back home. After getting over the jet lag I complained to British Airways about the stewards insolence and thoughtlessness and to the Travel Agent for their bungling of many factors which had put a sad note into our holiday.

We were refunded a considerable amount of money from the tour operator, regarding the incorrect Hotel rooms. I gave it all to Valerie, she needed it more me. There were many times she had been humiliated and almost treated as an inferior citizen who was not worth talking to or helping. She seemed to behave as this was normal, but I can assure you that I was not as calm as she was. All that British Airways would do was to send us both Wine and Flowers. Not a lot of good really, but at least some gesture was made. My gesture was not so polite. This was another visit for us both to remember, sometimes, for not the right reasons. We had visited 5 states. Wyoming. Montana, Nebraska, Colorado and Dakota.

Nice to be home though with many memories to share and yet another dream under my belt.

Chapter Five
AUSCHWITZ REMEMBERED.
This Is A Trip To Remember.

1995 was a year of mixed emotions, but I am glad to be able to share this experience. My eldest son had received a managerial promotion and been asked to move to Warsaw. His main task was to ensure that the Polish aircraft engineers maintained the Delta standards of safety. Of course being the dutiful Mother that I am, (and nosy) I wanted to visit him in his flat to make sure he was coping with this rather different change to his life. My sister was always as nosy as me so the two of us planned a visit. I was somewhat taken aback when my son readily agreed without any complaints.

On arrival at Gatwick airport we were somewhat surprised at the lack of queues for checking in, customs and passport control. This was great. We only suffered one small concern when a B.A official said, "Where is Poland?" You can probably guess that we told him, politely, of course. During the flight I asked the stewardess if I could visit the flight deck, and to prove my innocent intentions; I produced my flight crew membership card. I felt very privileged to be allowed into the cockpit and talk to both pilots. No food was served during this short flight but as I was hungry the air stewardess gave me her lunch. I told you so. It's not what you know but who. Things are no longer the same relaxed atmosphere on board an aircraft are they? On landing in Warsaw, we finally

45

located my son in the arrivals hall and after the customary greetings, we clambered into his very small hire car and drove to his flat. The journey took us through the outskirts of Warsaw and through the most depressing jungle of enormous concrete flats. Fortunately my son's flat was further into the newer greener suburbs and despite "quaint" plumbing and electrical installations, was pleasant and well appointed. I would dearly have loved to feminize his apartment but I know this would not be allowed. By early evening we were all getting hungry so with a well drawn map by my son, my sister and I walked off alone to find a supermarket.

Food shopping here is so different to what we are both used to. By 7.00.p.m. there were very orderly queues with no one complaining. The stock of food was quite small; the numbers of shopping baskets were rationed per person, very little lighting and few staff. Despite all of this everyone was calm, good natured and on hearing us speak in English became very helpful to us. We bought some food, paid the bill in Zloty returned to the flat, cooked the meal, watched T.V and finally exhausted, fell into bed.

By the morning after breakfast and ablutions we were ready to explore. The tour my son would take us on would be N.E. of Warsaw. En route we passed the Russian, Swiss and U.S. Embassies plus the Kings Palace which had been rebuilt after 1945. The Edifice, built by the Russians and known as the Palace of Culture, Science and Technology loomed large on the skyline looking rather out of place. This building is not a favourite of the Poles.

The farmlands were a surprise. The only power available appeared to be the horse and man's muscle. Sowing and hoeing was done by hand, by both men and women. By the end of day we felt that standing upright would be painful. What an eye opener this was. The scene was, in our opinion more typical of Africa.

By lunch time we are looking for food and finally found a small bar. The proprietor spoke only Polish and we spoke only English, so how to order food became a task. We finally ate chicken, chips and the Polish version of coleslaw all washed down with Pepsi. The meal was served in a very friendly manner in an impeccable eating house. A highlight of the day for us was seeing the storks flying in to begin their nesting season, plus birds of prey hovering over the countryside with their very distinctive hooked beaks clearly visible. That evening we were being taken out for a meal in the old town with my son's multinational buddies. Nationalities present were, English, American, German and Polish nationals. Communicating was to say the least, entertaining. After a very good meal we were taken to a jazz club in the old rebuilt city. What a fabulous evening we had.

The next day without too much trouble the exit from Warsaw was found and we drove W.N.W. alongside the forest where thousands of Poles were shot during the 2nd world war. Emotions here became a bit strained. Driving through some small towns we were surprised to see how many people were dressed in their National costume for church and how many had to take part in the service whilst outside on the church steps due to overcrowding. What are we doing wrong in England? We drove through

46

a town called Wola where the greatest single battle between the Polish and German armies took place. This was a history lesson with a difference. On the way to a place called Plock we found ourselves in a beautiful region of lakes surrounded by pine forests. As everything closes on a Sunday in Poland, trying to find somewhere to eat became a challenge. But true British grit came into play and we finally found a café and ordered, with some difficulty and amusement from Polish onlookers, soup, a smoked sausage, chips and ice cream. I expect you are now quite envious of our achievements in ordering food in Polish. Understanding the money is still somewhat of a problem. 5,000, 000 Zloty is worth approximately £125.00 and 1,000 Zloty = 2 and a half pence. I think that I would never work this out, too many noughts for me. On arriving in Wyszogrod we had the privilege to drive across the longest wooden bridge in Europe. As you can imagine there is a weight restriction, where only one car at a time is allowed to cross. Whilst crossing the bridge in the car, the quaint creaking and movement was to say the least, fascinating. After a long, tiring but wonderful day, supper was served and our beds began to call.

The next day we have planned to stay in the capital to see the sights of Warsaw. Our first stop was to visit the very large football stadium which houses the daily markets. Some of the stalls are manned by itinerant Russians. The clothes for sale were not too bad but the Russian wares consisted of everything from fake and or genuine icons, to knives, night vision binoculars and would you believe surgical chest retractors and enormous white brassieres. The mind boggles here. By the time we had circumnavigated the entire stadium we all needed the usual offices. They were unfortunately the squat type, very clean, but very hard on the knees and the back; my son fared better than my sister and I. On leaving the stadium we had to walk at least two miles to find a pedestrian bridge to cross, to take us into the Old Town Square. Walking around the enclosing wall there were many monuments including the one to the young fighters of the 1944 uprising. Then next on the list was the tomb of the Unknown Soldier, housed in its original, but war damaged memorial and guarded by two uniformed soldiers. By the end of the day, my sister and I are now, planning for our journey to Krakow in two days time. This entailed obtaining rail tickets and a Hotel booking for one night. With the help of a Delta employee this was finally arranged and we were given explicit details on how to recognise in Polish the words "Platform 3"

Our next visit was to Wilanow Palace which was just a short walk away along roads that had grass edges and luckily, the weather was fine and warm. From the outside, the church looked magnificent. Suddenly we were ushered out of the door by a broom wielding Nun and directed us to the other door. The approach to the Castle, the grounds, the decorations and the magnolias were enticing, but to our dismay we discovered that everything was closed on Tuesdays. Guess what day it was? Yes you're right it was Tuesday. So not to be downhearted we wondered around the gardens sat and watched a Tern successfully fishing in the lake, whilst we too successfully fished into our picnic bag. After making a visit to the church we walked

47

Above; The tomb of the Unknown Warrior   *Below; Wilanow Palace*

home through a magnificent housing area which appeared to be protected like Fort Knox. As we approached the edge of the estate where my son lived we realised how well maintained and pleasant most of it was. After a well earned evening meal, my sister and I decided which pictures should hang where in the flat to make it look and feel like home. For once my son didn't

48

argue with me and let me have my way. I expect the moment I fly back to England he will reposition them all where he wants them.

Today was the big day. My son was due back at work at 7.00.a.m. and we would be left to get ourselves to Krakow.

After a shower and breakfast I managed to find out how to work the telephone and called for a taxi to take us to the station. We felt very proud of ourselves as we found Peron 3 which is platform 3 in English and boarded the 9.00.a.m. train and began looking for our booked seats in 1st class. We couldn't locate them, so we found an empty compartment and made ourselves comfortable. When the ticket collector came around he asked, "Why are you in 2nd class when you have tickets for 1st class?" We now knew why we didn't find our booked seats; we were in the wrong part of the train. He was very kind and told us that we could stay where we were. After all why should he care if we travel 2nd class with a 1st class ticket? After 3 hours covering very flat boring countryside we were nearing Krakow. The weather was decidedly "iffy" and we of course had packed nothing but summer wear and didn't even have an umbrella between us. What could we do? So….. We walked in the pouring rain, getting strange looks from passers by, to the nearest taxi rank where we were soon delivered to the Ibis Hotel (French owned). On the surface, things looked good. How wrong can you be sometimes? What is it with me? Things always seem to happen. Ah well it always makes a good story. According to the booking clerk we had only been allocated a single room. With a good degree of mutterings about the booking clerk and the Delta friend who had placed the booking, things began to change for the better. We finally forgave everyone and after settling into our newly allocated room we went back to the receptionist and booked a trip down a Salt mine for that same afternoon. The second trip would be to Auschwitz and Birkenau for the following day. By now we were both ravishing and very wet, so the first thing we did was to try to find a shop where we could buy an umbrella. We also had to find a restaurant as the hotel was not serving food due to a large conference being held there. We feel a bit sorry for ourselves at the moment and rather alone in a country where we are unable to speak or understand the language. But, hey, we are now going to the salt mine, this will be good. The salt mines were something very special, like the descent by steps to well over 100 metres or 300 feet. The digging had begun in prehistoric times and still continues today. There were many fine sculptures, friezes, chandeliers, stairways and churches all cut out of solid salt, mostly for the enjoyment of the tourists. It was very hard to believe that these were made from salt. The final test came when descending a very large staircase with handrails, all of which were made from salt. When no one was looking I licked the stairway handrail. You're right, it is made of salt. Ugh. Getting to the surface was for the hardy. 10 of us were literally crammed into a miner's cage, all lights extinguished and we were whipped to the surface travelling at 4 metres per second. I have to say that most of us screamed as we ascended. I was never so glad before to see daylight and get out of the cage. I wanted to buy some salt from the shop but due to the late hour, they were closed. You can't win 'em all can you?

Lying in bed that night we were both thinking about our next days' excursion to Auschwitz. We had talked about it the previous day, and we both thought about it once or twice during the night, but nothing can prepare you for your breadth of emotions. The size of Birkenau is memorable and terrible as an extermination camp. We both found it impossible to empathise with men, women and children, forced to live, even for a few weeks in freezing conditions. Their room infested with rats, starving and sleeping 20 to a bed of straw, designed for 2 and never knowing at which point they would be taken to the gas chambers. Different parts of the camp elicited anger, at what man can do to man; fear, that it could have been us or that it could happen again; shame that it ever did happen; shock at the size of this institutionalised mass murder and disbelief that what we had been told was true about this cold calculated terror. Some exhibits evinced more emotion than others. A room full of babies and toddlers shoes, tons and tons

The gas chambers

of human hair, some of the ribbons still attached to plaits. The punishment block made our blood run cold. If anyone had been caught sharing their bread, this is where they were sent to their very slow, cold painful death. The women were stripped naked and put into a black underground concrete hole without food, sanitation or warmth. There were two to a cell and it was impossible to sit or lie down. Here they were left to die of cold, starvation and despair. Perhaps something even more moving was the fact that on the very day of our visit, Israel commemorated the 50th Anniversary of the liberation of all the Nazi camps. To support this epic episode, Jewish citizens from many parts of the world had gathered at Auschwitz.They wore blue jackets and caps bearing the Star of David and marched behind the Jewish flag in total silence, men, women, children, young and old. By the time the very last person had walked past us, which took some 25 minutes, my sister and I were crying aloud uncontrollably. Because parts of the camp were taken over by the Jewish community for remembrance and prayers, we were unable to see the death camps from the vantage point of the entrance tower, but the sound of Jewish songs reached us from the gas chambers area some 800 yards away as we stood shivering in the freezing rain by the railway lines of Birkenau. We were fully clothed, not naked as the new arrivals were. How could this have ever happened?

Before finally leaving this horrendous place we actually went into the gas chambers and visited the crematoriums. That day will live in my memory forever, and all I did was visit as a tourist. There are still survivors who make a pilgrimage once a year and stay in apartments just outside the camp. There is still something very eerie about the location of this torture

The Crematorium Ovens

camp. The surrounding area seems to be dead of all living things. We never heard or saw a bird, there seemed to be no flowers in the fields and nothing alive.

Back at our hotel we sat in silence for the rest of the day. There seemed to be nothing that we could say that was worthwhile. After a very fitful and sleepless night we packed our bags and made ready for the train journey back to Warsaw.

We thought whilst we are here in Krakow lets take a last look around. So, armed with a map, having settled the Hotel bill we walked to the centre and soon found the Cloth Hall markets. This is a collection of stalls selling Polish made artefacts, where we both bought a few mementos for the folks back home. We both now urgently needed the usual offices and to this end we found a café where we could not only have a drink but satisfy our other needs. Unfortunately, I have been coughing and suffering a very sore throat for some days now. Our waitress spoke fairly good English, even enough to make a joke. She said she was sorry to hear that I had the Krakow (w pronounced V) cough. Suddenly another customer came over to our table and said, "Oh boy you're English can I speak to you to practice the language?" How could we refuse she was so friendly? After a few pleasantries had been exchanged, she enquired whether this was our first visit to Poland and to her wonderful city of Krakow. On replying in the affirmative she told us that we could not possibly leave the square until we had witnessed the altar opening on the hour in the Cathedral and listened to the music which was, she said," The best in Europe". So being very British, stiff upper lip and all that, we took her advice and although the opening of the altar doors were really beautiful we were unmoved by the music. In fact it was so short that it hardly registered at all.

From the Cathedral we walked to the Kazimierz, a Jewish sector of Krakow which had been occupied since the 14th century. This ghetto had been emptied by the Germans in 1943 and it still looked as if the people had just left. The tenement blocks joined with very dark passages, were there, just like we had always seen in films when the Nazis took away the Jews. In fact this area evoked the same feelings in us as we had experienced in Auschwitz. We asked ourselves many times, why are the Jews always treated as 2nd class citizens? We also learned that from here, Jews were taken to a camp at Plaszow, which was the site of Schindlers factories? We then walked in silence to get back to our Hotel, and with a bit of help from friendly Polish citizens, we made it. After completing all our business we took a taxi to the station and spent a rather complex time trying to ascertain where to go and which train to get on. By a process of elimination we plumped for the correct train, but there were still many doubts creeping in on the 3 hour ride back to Warsaw. Back in my son's flat he enquired as to where we had been and what we had seen.Upon relaying the story to him that we had gone alone into a Jewish ghetto, he was appalled and told us that what we had done, was a highly dangerous area to go into alone. If only we had known. But fortunately for us, we came out in one piece. The next day we flew back home to England. My visit to Poland will remain in my memory for ever. Even the children of Poland will also not be allowed to forget. At the age of 13, part of the school curriculum is to visit the camp at Auschwitz. To this day I find it impossible to watch any television programme about Auschwitz, it is too emotional. My sister and I were only visitors and it will always, for me, remain impossible to comprehend what it must be like for the few survivors and family of those who suffered such barbarism.

But, yet again, something else achieved in "To do list". In my opinion this visit should be made compulsory to all and sundry. Finally, even when I read my own chapter on this subject I can still cry and become emotional. My very small scars will remain with me forever.

Chapter Six

THE WAR IS NOW OVER.

At the age of 75 I can clearly remember V.J. night, with street parties, food and singing. It was at this time that I made my first ever public performance.
To earn 10 shillings worth of savings stamps I sang. "You are my sunshine my only sunshine". Unfortunately I got the words wrong, but they still paid me. I sang, "Came Miss Illusion, instead of "This illusion". Do you know it was over 20 years later when I finally realised what I had sung?

I am now 8 years old and at the moment still living in Morden with Granny, waiting to be re-housed. I had my first boy friend here. I can even remember his name, it was Clive. We used to play kiss chase and I would always let him catch me, as you do.
Many years later upon visiting Granny, I saw this very smart young man in his army uniform walking towards me. Yep, it was Clive, I immediately recognised him. I smiled at him and said "Hello". He blushed to the roots and ran indoors rather hurriedly. I have often wondered what on earth we used to do in the bushes after I had let him catch me. His memory must be better than mine.
We have at last now been re housed in a council house in Balham.
My Auntie Ethel, who was my Grandmothers sister, lived upstairs and the downstairs was ours, for Mum, my sister and I. This consisted of a Scullery, a very small toilet, 2 bedrooms and a room which we then called the kitchen, but today would be called the lounge. The only heating was a black range, a coal fire, or paraffin heaters. During the then, very cold winters, our bedroom windows were covered on the inside with very pretty frosty patterns. Sometimes it was even necessary to put a paraffin heater in the toilet. Soft toilet tissue had not been invented yet so we had to use Jeyes very shiny toilet paper. If you have a vivid imagination here it would be very helpful.

I have to be honest, not having a Father living at home with us was very hard, when all your friends around you would talk about the day out they had with their Dad.

Neighbours can be very unkind. We were unfortunate to have one, who was very nosy. One day she stopped me on my way to school and asked me, "Why are their no gentlemen's underpants on your clothes line on Mondays?" Being a quick thinker I actually replied, "Mum is very embarrassed about these articles being shown to all the neighbours, so she only hangs them on the line at night time".

One incident will live with me forever. You know when you're a child that your Mother would never swear? Monday wash day arrived as usual, all the whites were boiled, rinsed and mangled and hung on the clothes line, which stretched the length of the garden, with one of those lovely natural wooden Y shaped props made by the local gypsies. Sometime mid morning, the clothes line broke, depositing all the whites onto the muddy garden path. Mum muttered something under her breath, repaired the clothes line with a granny knot, bought all the whites indoors and started again. The second time the line broke; Mum's demeanour seemed to get a bit more agitated, but still no nasty words. You can probably guess the next bit of excitement as finally for the third time the line broke again, putting all the pristine whites back into the mud. Mum rushed into the garden fuming, she then jumped on top of all the washing in the mud and proceeded to grind them further into the ground whilst shouting for all to hear, Sod, Bugger, Dam, Blast, Shit.

I had never heard such words before and least of all from your Mother.

I learnt that everyone has a breaking point and Mum had reached hers. I was now told in no uncertain terms, "You will now help me with the washing".

In our scullery we had a concrete boiler heated by wood and coke. So, I was sent into the garden to chop some small firewood to get the boiler started. As soon as the clean water was boiling the whites were thrown in and stirred around with the now famous copper stick. When this process was finished the whites were removed with washing tongs and placed into the round tin bath in the Butler sink to be rinsed. Next step was to ring by hand as much water out as was humanly possible, and then the two of us would fold the sheets very carefully, pulling on the opposite corners to keep the sheets square. The next step was the mangle. We owned

Cast-iron mangle with large wooden wheels

one of those very large old mangles with two large wooden rollers. My job was to turn the enormous handle to get the rollers revolving whilst Mum carefully fed the sheets through avoiding getting her fingers caught.

Another of my designated jobs was to polish all the brass door knobs, polish the very heavy duty lino with Lavender floor polish and then buff to a high shine. Iron the hankies and anything that was straight and uncomplicated and finally go shopping Friday afternoon after school for the groceries for the weekend.

In those days we were brought up to be a "doer". No T.V. no mobiles, no video games or computers, our fun came in a different package.
We did not have a fridge so all the food was stored in the passageway as this was the coldest spot in the house. Bulk buying was not an option in our family, for two reasons, not enough money and no fridge.

Sometimes just to keep my sister and I happy, we would sit round the fire and sing songs, one of which I still remember today.

Today's Monday, today's Monday, Monday is washing day, is everybody happy? You bet your life we are.
Today's Tuesday. Today's Tuesday, Tuesday soup, is everybody happy? You bet your life we are.
Today's Wednesday, Today's Wednesday, Wednesday Roast Beef, is everybody happy? You bet your life we are.
Today's Thursday. Today's Thursday, Thursday Shepherds Pie, is everybody happy? You bet your life we are.
Today's Friday, Today's Friday, Friday Fish, is everybody happy? You bet your life we are.
Today's Saturday, Today's Saturday, Saturday is Pay Day, is everybody happy? You bet your life we are.
Today's Sunday, Today's Sunday, Sunday Church, is everybody happy? You bet your life we are.

I can imagine there are many of you out there who have sung this song.

Things slowly began to improve; there were no more bombs falling and no more of my school friends being killed. Food and clothing was still rationed, but at least we all felt safe.

Friday night was Amami

The New Ascot water heater, real luxury.

Help Yourself To **HOT WATER**

whenever you like with GAS and the Ascot Sink Heater. Instantly ready at a turn of the tap and continuous supply for as long as you want it. No work, no waiting and no waste.

Available on Easy Hire Purchase Terms

ASCOT SINK GAS WATER HEATER

BRISTOL GAS COMPANY
RADIANT HOUSE   ·   BRISTOL 1

The Old Tin Bath
night, and this is how it worked in our council house. We had been lucky enough to have an Ascot water heater fitted in the scullery, so hot water was at the turn of a tap.

The next job was to take the round tin bath from the wall in the garden, wash out the dirt and the spiders and place it on the scullery stone floor near the Ascot. Once the hose was attached and the water turned on, the bath was very slowly filled with hot water. Being no heat in the scullery, the gas oven was lit and the door left open.Mum, being Mum, had the privilege of taking of the waters first to wash her hair and bathe.

My sister was next, as she is older than me, to do the same. By now it's my turn; the water is a bit colder and no longer looking as clean as it once had been, but I was allowed to top it up with some more hot water. I had to sit cross legged to enable me to fit in the very small bath. On many occasions I decided to unravel my legs and place them in the oven, until they began to cook. Anyone fancy a medium rare leg?
Once I was clean I called for Mum who would wash my hair for me.
The use of a plastic jug was the only method of rinsing away the soap.
Then when my ablutions were finally finished and I was clean, dry and in my nightdress ready for bed, this was when the next major job became available for all hands on deck. Getting ready to empty the bath.
It took the three of us to lift and drag the bath full of water to the back door, lift it up over the step and poor the contents into the outside drain, clean the bath and hang it once more in its resting place until next Friday, when all of this would be repeated.

Mum always used to make a cheese and potato pie which was ready on completion of our Friday night expedition. We would sit on the floor in front of the black range and eat until nothing was left, except the crusty bits round the edge of the dish. If like all youngsters we were often still hungry, the next treat was crumpets and some of our butter ration.
Out would come the extending toasting fork, stick a crumpet on the prongs and toast it by the heat of the range.
I miss these times, we are too regimented these days, with things that we now switch on and so many jobs are done for you. It's not the same as

hands on. Nothing can compare with the smell of freshly toasted crumpets in front of an open fire. Not the same smell when done in a toaster. I remember very clearly those lovely Friday nights with my hair in metal hair curlers or Kirby grips, sitting on the floor, being warm, eating Mum's cooking and listening to the wireless.

My favourite programmes were Dick Barton special agent with Jock and Snowy, Paul Temple, Peter Brough and Archie Andrews, Arthur Askey, Valentine Dial, Wilfred Pickles and Tommy Hanley, Mrs Mop and "Can I do you now Sir?" Do you remember Rob Wilton's catch phrase? "The day war broke out, my missus said to me". I know there are many many more which you will remember. Why not have some fun now and try to sing the signature tunes and share this information with your family.
I'll leave a space here so that you can fill in any other programmes you might remember.

As a young child, trying to sleep with curlers digging into your scalp was practically impossible. This torture was endured all in the cause of making you look more beautiful. But…..by the morning half the curlers had fallen out during fitful tossing and turning, so one side of your hair was still very curly but the other side was now flat as a pancake and completely straight. All this trouble had been for nothing as the hair now had to be washed again in a hurry ready for school.

I bet you can all remember Nitty Nora. For those not able to do so, she was the Nurse who visited the schools to test the pupils to see if they had nits. I was lucky enough not to be infected but unfortunately my sister not so. She had nits. When she came home from school she was very upset by the news, after all we were a very clean family. We now know this has nothing to do with whether you can be infected or not. Both Mum and I felt very sorry for her, so to cheer her up we took her to the Odeon picture house at Clapham South. Guess what the film was called, "This happy breed" staring Celia Johnson and Robert Newton. As a family we will always remember that film with a giggle, particularly my sister.

Another medical problem that seemed to be rife at that time was "Worms" which infested your intestines and bowels and caused quite a bit of discomfort, itching and unpleasantness.

The treatment for worms was as follows: This began with a visit from the local District Nurse. The dining room table was covered in a waterproof sheet and a towel in preparation for what was about to happen. The Nurse then filled a large old aluminium jug with boiling water and into this was placed the "cure" which was called Quasher Chips. These were small pieces of cream coloured bark from the Liquorice tree. Does this tell you something?
The second piece of "torture" was a long black rubber tube with a soft round shaped ball half way down the length of the said tube. The "rubber

gloves" were then put on and all was ready for the procedure. Next it was my turn to get ready. I had to remove all under garments and lay on my side with knees up and the correct part of my body in readiness. One end of the rubber tube was ceremoniously inserted into my back passage whilst the other end was placed into the large jug containing the "Quasher chips" solution, which by now had cooled and was pronounced ready. Do you all remember what the old blood pressure equipment looked like with the rubber shaped ball halfway down the black tubing, and how this was used? Well, the black ball is now being squeezed rather rapidly emptying the contents of this 2 litre jug of liquid into my bottom. I hope you all have a vivid imagination at this point. My stomach is expanding very rapidly and I am in vain trying to hold on to what I am told not to let go just yet. Not easy. When at last, all the liquid had passed through the tube and into my derriere, I usually screamed at this point, leapt of the dining room table and unceremoniously emptied the vast quantity of liquid into two chambers. The next unenviable task for the Nurse was to sift through the contents to see how many worms where still visible. If there were none the treatment had finished. If there were still some visible, the same procedure would be undertaken the following week.

I hope you all,, who are reading this vital piece of information, are glad you were not born in my era. Today the treatment is easier, one or two tablets will suffice.

I have now reached the ripe age of 11 in 1949. Much to my Mother's surprise and mine I passed my 11 plus to a Grammar School called Rosa Bassett School for young ladies. I was not!!!

Being very good at sport and gymnastics I had the privilege to be chosen to be a ball boy/girl for the Wimbledon trials which were held in Surbiton.

One well known player which had the pleasure of my ball girling skills was that fabulous player John Newcombe. He had such wonderful legs, long and full of muscles, the like I had never seen before.

I didn't enjoy my time at this Grammar School; they were too clever for me; the subjects we had to study were; English Language. English Literature. Maths, Algebra. Geometry. Physics. Science Chemistry. Biology. History. Geography. Domestic Science. Gymnastics. Tennis. Netball. Hockey. Swimming. French. German. Latin and finally Greek.

How could any child of 12 years old manage to understand all of these subjects? I can clearly remember performing Pyramus and Thisbee in Latin. The only word I can now still say, from this performance is: "Sanguinalentum", which means covered in blood.

I know you must feel very proud to have learnt such a lot by reading this chapter!!!!!

Our geography teacher was not very popular, she was very strict. No one dared to speak during her lessons unless asked to do so. Our class decided that she needed to be punished. So on the designated day I bought into class 2 very strong kippers and proceeded to tie them behind the revolving blackboard in her classroom. The month was June and fortunately or unfortunately the weather was superb. Are you ahead of me?

It was only after 3 or 4 days that a very pungent smell began to permeate the classroom which was evacuated and further entry was not allowed. The school was buzzing with health inspectors and our Janitor, who were trying to determine the source of the pong which was now accompanied by hoards of bluebottles and maggots. Finally the offending objects were found, eliminated and the room fumigated. The guilty party or parties were then questioned heavily. Finally as I stood up and admitted that I was the culprit, the entire class of girls also stood up and accepted the blame. We were all given detention every night for a week and made to write out each afternoon 100 times,

"I must not hang kippers behind the blackboard in the classroom of the geography teacher".

During my time at the Grammar School, Mum had, in my opinion become very strange. The least little thing seemed to send her over the edge, and as I was usually the "Least little thing", it was deemed my fault which caused her outbursts of violence.

Being a tom boy I was always up a tree or climbing on something causing my clothes to tear. As you can imagine clothing was still rationed and replacing my torn garments was far too expensive. Most of the time I did my best to hide the tear with a well placed hand or anything suitable.

Once the rent in my clothes had been discovered I begged my Mum not to hit me anymore to no avail. The punishment was metered out with our Dad's sergeant major army swagger stick which was bound at one end with waxed string. This stick was applied to my back until her temper had died down.

My sister would lie on top of me during the punishment to help shield me from the worst. If it was my sister's turn I would do the same. Sometimes if the army stick wasn't near to hand the copper stick was used or a well placed slap or punch with a fist around my head, leaving wheels clearly visible.One day I had badly torn my winter coat, and I did not want to suffer anymore pain. Luckily we had an Auntie Minnie next door who was very good at invisible darning. It was 6 days before Mum noticed the darn and then the fire had gone out of her so no beating on that occasion.

To escape from my Mother: being a very resourceful young lady I built myself a tree house in the back garden. As she could not climb up to me I knew I would be safe until her temper had died down. When the weather was too bad for me to hide in the garden I used to lock myself in the only toilet for at least 6 hours, making Mum go next door to use the facilities, thereby making her tell a fib as to why she could not use her own toilet.

Whilst still at my Grammar school getting changed for the netball lesson, the teacher wondered where I was and came looking for me. I always got changed after all the other girls had departed not wanting anyone to see the wheels on my back. Just as I am taking the jumper over my head the teacher arrived and saw the marks. She was devastated and immediately wanted to take my sister and I and put us into care. I fought her verbally tooth and nail and told her that both my sister and I were happier with the devil we knew rather than one we didn't know. So all was kept quiet.

By the age of 16 I had had enough of her violence. One day whilst sitting at the dining room table, I must have given her a bit of cheek as teenagers do. She suddenly came at me with fists flying and punched me around the head, knocking my head against the wall and rendering me unconscious. When I came too with my head in the plate of bread, butter and jam, I sized up to her and said, "That is the last time you ever lay a hand on me".

You have probably guessed by now, that made her even angrier. I put my hands up to protect myself and punched the homing in fist. This broke her thumb and I had to take her to the hospital. When the surgeon enquired as to what had happened she said, "I fell over in the snow". She never laid another angry hand on me after that.

Chapter Seven

THESE EXPERIENCES SHAPED MY LIFE

This chapter puts together a few stories which I think helped me become the person I am. Sometimes good, sometimes naughty, sometimes frightening and most of the time these happenings have helped me be the person that I am.

I've already told you that both my parents were Migraine sufferers which I inherited from the age of 11. In those days there was no medical help except aspirins. For fellow sufferers, you know that these are no help at all. My Migraines would start without any warnings. Split vision for 20 minutes, pain that has to be endured to understand, vomiting for up to 8 hours, sometimes mild convulsions, and mild paralysis, when tested, no reflexes at all, plus not being able to tell which way was up, therefore very giddy. My Father had a way of trying to help me through the pain. "Always remember my girl, only highly intellectual people get Migraines". It worked for a while but now I know that is not true. At one point in my life things became so bad that I actually tried to jump out of my bedroom window making it vitally important for my Doctor to visit me and put me out with a Pethadin injection, which very quickly I became addicted to. I finally confessed to this problem and together we managed to wean me off this drug which took 6 weeks of quite hard and determined work.

Sometime later I was given my own Fermagin injections to help alleviate the pain during an attack. Fermagin was made from the mould of rye and helped enlarge the blood vessels leading to the head helping to reduce that throbbing pain, which I must say worked very well for many years. One day when I requested a repeat of this drug, I was told that "This can cause side effects, so we have taken it off the market". If only these people who make these decisions could have a Migraine attack they would realise that any side effect would be better than a Migraine. But

61

there you go it's health and safety at it again. So far in my life time nothing else has ever been as effective.

By now I was experiencing three or four attacks per week, so I was taken to Atkinson Morley Hospital in Wimbledon, which specialised in injuries to the head to see if there was anything else wrong with me: like a tumour or lack of a brain. Luckily there was no tumour and I am told that they are still looking to find a brain. During my time in this hospital I was "lucky" enough to have an attack which made all the consultants very excited to be able to witness what they called a Classic Migraine attack. A large number of trainee consultants were brought along to study me. I felt like a piece of meat, but if this would help others I was prepared to suffer on one condition only. When they have all finished I wish to be put to sleep so as not to feel anymore pain. Luckily that is just what they did. Just because I was in hospital, it wasn't a trauma. I was in a mixed ward with 4 men and myself. All of us were as you might say, NOT ILL just needing some tests, so during the day we were fully dressed and we only had to get into something more SEXY when it was our turn for the next test. The fellows I shared my room with were horse racing fanatics and so very quickly I too learnt to put on a bet and see if I could win a fortune. You can probably guess that during one week I won at least enough to buy a Mars bar for myself and my INMATES. As you can imagine, not being ill as such, time lagged very badly.

One afternoon our Nigerian male nurse must have also been bored as he came into our ward for some conversation. Mind you he was the one who provided it so we just sat and listened.

He started by telling us where he came from and that his Father was the chief of his tribe. We all bowed and scraped just to show our allegiance to his tribe. The local custom was that when the boy child of the chief became 13 years old he was sent to live with his Grand parents to not only help them as they grew older and less capable, but for them to impart their life time of knowledge and skill to the male chief who would be next in line. Oh how I wish we could have all done the same in our civilisation. So at the age of 13 years our male nurse was sent to live with his Grand parents on their chicken farm in the backwoods of Nigeria. One afternoon when all the work was done for the time being, Granddad told his Grandson, "Why don't you go and play with some of your friends and I will see you at supper time?" One of their favourite games was to catch a large rat, just for fun. The rat runs would be located and the boys would block up all, bar one hole with wet mud. Straws would be drawn to see who would be fortunate or unfortunate enough to be the lucky one to wait by the one remaining open hole to catch the rat with his hands. You know who it was don't you? All the other boys now lie on top of the rat runs and begin to pound with their hands and feet to frighten the rats to run, whilst our nurse is lying down in front of the only open hole vigilant as ever, with his hands cupped ready. The young boys start to yell, "It's coming, and we can hear it".Terrified but ready, the pounding gets nearer, the boys yell out,"NOW". At this instant our nurse cupped his hands over the hole and grabbed what he thought was a rat. Unfortunately it was not a rat, but a large snake which he now had by the neck and he was too terrified to let it go. There was panic amongst the boys, but they sent one youngster back to find Granddad to tell him what had transpired and to be ready. The boys now formed a straight line some distance behind the boy with the snake and made their way back to the chicken farm, some quietly screaming and some crying hysterically. On arrival at the farm Granddad was there waiting with a large forked stick ready to do something with the snake. All the boys were told to run away and hide in the barn leaving just our nurse, the snake and his faithful Granddad. Our nurse was told that on the count of three, drop the snake and run. As he did so the snake fell to the ground very dead. It had been throttled by the young Grandson who in terror had gripped it so tightly. All was well that ended well.

His second story was every bit as amusing. Granddad was losing quite a lot of chickens to the local cobras, so he told his Grandson, that tonight he would teach him how to alleviate this problem. He was told to boil some eggs all day to make sure they were solid.

That evening after dark both granddad and grand son went to the chicken coup to perform this dark and dirty deed. The two of them are now sitting in the pitch dark in the chicken run with Granddad armed with a rifle and our nurse with the eggs. He still does not know why he had to boil these eggs. When a cobra wants to eat an egg, as you are aware they have no teeth and cannot chew, so they sidle up to an egg swallow it and then rear up with their neck against a wooden pole and hit their neck until the egg breaks and then they can swallow. Are you following this story so far? In the centre of the chicken run Granddad had erected a wooden pole. He then instructed his Grandson to place the very hard boiled eggs around the base. They then both sat very quietly and waited; our nurse told us that he was terrified. Suddenly this enormous cobra sidled under the netting and made straight for the eggs, swallowed them all then reared up with his neck against the pole and tried to break the eggs. As you can imagine this was not possible and the cobra killed himself trying. What a great story. It saved having to use any bullets and saved all the chickens from an untimely death.

So you see, not all hospital stays are boring or bad for you. This visit gave me a good few stories that will stay with me for a long time.

•   •   •

I don't know where to start next to relive some of my exploits and to be able to share them. All I can say is read my stories and then start to recall some of your own for the benefit of your family.

The last holiday that I took with Mum started out to be quite ordinary. We were going to Shanklin on the Isle of Wight, taking the ferry from Portsmouth to Ryde. The sailing was smooth and trouble free. On arrival in the harbour, every one was standing up with cases ready to disembark. The sharp end of the ship, ooops sorry, the bow was attached to the jetty, with the blunt end oh sorry, the stern slowly being pulled into place. I am standing ready to get off and there is a very pregnant lady in front of me holding her small son's hand. On looking up, I noticed a very large paddle steamer coming towards us at quite a remarkable turn of speed. I pointed this out to Mum who told me not to worry he can obviously see us, we are quite large. The Captain on the bridge of our ferry was shouting words I had never heard before, to the Captain of the paddle steamer. The paddle steamer was not slowing down one iota and finally hit the stern of our ferry at full speed. Every one on board was immediately thrown backwards. I caught the pregnant lady who fell on top of me. I think I saved her unborn baby. Her small son fell and cut his mouth very badly on the seats. As you can imagine chaos is now raining supreme. A large chunk of the jetty was ripped away with our ferry still attached to one end. I found this quite exciting to be involved in a collision of two large sea vessels. Help very quickly arrived in the form of Doctors and Nurses to help the injured. On land this did not appear to be under control. I don't think that anything like this had ever happened before and no one seemed to know what to do next. Although it would have been possible to disembark, this was not allowed. So for over two hours we remained on board whilst the ferry rocked very slowly from side to side. At no time were we, as passengers, ever given any information as to what was going to transpire. Everyone on board was now very sea sick due to the very steady rocking motion, causing even more upset all round. Sick bags were in abundance.

We were all very relieved when we at last were allowed to disembark and begin our fun time on the I.O.W. Somehow everything after that seemed quite dull.

•   •   •

1955 November 5th is a date that is burnt, (in more ways than one) permanently into my brain. You can tell from the date mentioned, this was bonfire night. Money was still very scarce and my cousin Michael and I wanted our own firework display. We borrowed a wheelbarrow and knocked on every door in our street and asked for old newspapers or magazines. At the end of our road was a MAN who collected these items and paid tuppence a lb. Pretty soon there were no old newspapers left anywhere in our road. Even then we were helping with re-cycling, but we didn't know it. Having saved enough money we toddled off to the firework shop to make our very own purchases. Roman candles, 3ft rockets, double sized jumping crackers, large Catherine wheels, bangers and sparklers, plus anything else we could afford. On bringing them home we placed all of them on the dining room table in a circle, small ones in the centre, getting bigger as the circle grew. The 3 foot rockets we lent against the table and the roman candles were around the edge of the table with the blue touch papers sticking out. The jumping crackers were placed next to the roman candles. What a sight, we felt so proud of our achievements. We had done this all on our own without any financial help from the adults. Whilst standing there and staring, my sister and her husband appeared. We very proudly showed off our exhibits, and extended an invitation to watch our display that night. My Brother-in-Law, being a smoker, one of those, roll yer own sort, was leaning over the table smoking. You can probably guess where this story is leading. Yes, you're right, the end fell off his cigarette and fell onto the very large Roman candle, which then ignited the jumping crackers, Catherine wheels, sparklers and finally the 3 foot rockets shot upwards, hitting the ceiling. My sister and I screamed, as my Brother-in-Law swept all the lit fireworks into his arms and ran to the scullery, threw them into the butler sink, whilst I turned on all the taps to not only extinguish the fireworks but the brave man's chest as well. We then both realised that my sister was still in the room with the fireworks, she hadn't managed to escape. We grabbed some towels, soaked them in water and crawled back into the living room. The sight was terrifying, There were ceiling high flames giving off tremendous heat, visibility was zero as the room was enveloped in multi coloured smoke. We screamed my sister's name. She was trapped behind the table. We covered our heads with the wet towels, threw one over my sister and dragged her to safety. My Brother-in-Law then went back into the maelstrom with buckets of water and extinguished the fire. Unfortunately my sister suffered burst blood vessels in her eyes and was taken to Hospital for treatment. Drawing breath we all tried to take in just what had happened. Should I be furious with my Brother-in-Law for spoiling our fun and sending all our hard earned cash up in smoke or should I just be glad that we are all still alive and not seriously hurt? The latter won. Mum's living room was black from floor to ceiling, the lino was scorched, a ten bob note that was on the sideboard had gone up in smoke and the table was, how can I describe this, well; it had seen better days and needed refurbishment. I was then given the unenviable task of walking to the factory where Mum worked and whilst walking her home, relate the afternoons exciting escapade. As it was raining I took with me a brolly. She was so pleased to see me and remarked how kind I was to come to meet her. Little did she know why I had been so kind? I then dropped the bombshell and ran away from her in a hurry so as not to get a clout. Her next reaction, for her, was unusual, she just said, "Oh dear how terrible, is every one O.K."? I thought that she might change her attitude when she sees the damage, but luckily she remained completely calm.

My sister and her husband totally repaired the kitchen, my sister's eye got better, but Bonfire night was, for my cousin and me a Damp Squid.

.   .   .

Living still in Balham we were very near to Tooting Bec Common and as I was still training to play my favourite game called Korfball, most evenings, if I was free, I would join my team mates over the common and we would train together until nearly dark. One such evening's episode will remain with me for life. Having finished our session, we all said goodbye and then made our individual way home. I slung the size 5 football back in its net and began the walk home across the common. During that time there was what was known as "The Balham Gang", a very violent hard nosed bunch of teenagers whose one aim in life was to "Hurt".

I saw them in the distance and as a young female alone I knew it was not safe to be seen. I ran in the opposite direction to them and hid amongst some trees. Fortunately for me they hadn't seen me. As they disappeared into the distance I knew I was safe, left my cover and rather shaken started my journey home. In the distance I could hear someone crying and screaming for help. I carefully followed the sound and to my horror I came upon a small boy of about 10 year's old hanging by a rope from a branch of a tree with a fire burning beneath him. Nothing in life can ever prepare you for such blatant cruelty. I kicked the fire away with my boots, climbed the tree and untied the rope to enable me to lower him to the ground. He was not burned but very shaken and frightened. I did my best to calm him down and then asked him where he lived so that I could make sure he got home safely. I finally delivered him safely to his Mum and Dad who thanked me for my bravery and care. They contacted the police and most of the members of the gang were prosecuted and punished, not enough in my opinion. If I had been a Judge I would have liked to meter out the same punishment as they had inflicted, just to let them feel the terror. But…. You can't do that can you? I'm told its AGAINST HUMAN RIGHTS. What a load of balderdash. We are as soft now as we were all those years ago.

•   •   •

There were other occasions when I was put in jeopardy; I think it had something to do with living in Balham. One evening walking home along Balham High Road with my netball in a bag over my shoulder, I had the distinct feeling that I was being followed. We girls seem to be able to sense this don't we? So I did what I was taught to do. I stopped to look into a shop window to see if the man in question would go past me. Of course he did. I said to myself "You see you were wrong, who on earth would want to follow you"? I then with a thankful heart turned down Hildreth Street, which during the day was a market with stalls selling food, but now at 10.00p.m it was quiet and empty. The man in question had now disappeared from my view. As I walked past the local bakers shop doorway, I had a premonition. I carefully wrapped the netball netting around my wrist in readiness to use it as a weapon if it was needed. As I drew level with the aforementioned doorway a man jumped out at me with his trousers down and thrusting his bits and pieces at me. The netball came in very handy. I swung it very fast and caught him where he did not wish to be caught. He screamed in pain, fell to his knees and whilst he was trying to pull up his trousers to follow me, I took off at speed. It is true what Confucius says. "Woman can run faster with skirts up than man can with trousers down. I never told my Mum what had happened. She would have said, "It was probably your fault, you encouraged him".
I might as well get all my unpleasant stories over in one go. So, come here, there's more.
Travelling on the underground every day to the city for work was quite a

daunting procedure. You are squashed very tightly together with people you have never met before, confined to a very small space, with the train making you rock backwards and forwards. On the day in question I am squashed into the train from Balham on my way to London Bridge, carrying a box bag. For those not familiar with this piece of equipment this is a small hard sided square box made to house your personal possessions such as purse, wallet, make up, sandwiches, nail varnish, a pair of stockings, a drink and a clean pair of knickers, just in case. I am strap hanging in a very crowded train in the rush hour and there is a gentleman to my right hand side. Suddenly I thought I could feel a cold hand on my stocking tops and my suspender was twanged. I knew it couldn't be me, both my hands were engaged, one holding the strap and one holding the box bag. (But then why would I twang my own suspender?) A gentleman in front of me obviously could see what was happening and mouthed the words, "Do you need help?" I replied, "I think I can deal with this thank you very much". As the train jerked, a space appeared between me and the pervert. I slowly moved my box bag to my left hand side. I then did the unthinkable; I used my bag as a battering ram to inflict some damage to the man with evil intentions. He fell to the floor of the train in some discernible discomfort, whilst quietly groaning. When the train arrived at the station, he crawled out on to the platform and lay there grovelling. Every one on the train applauded me for my courage. It was at this time that a small niggling doubt began to creep in. Suppose I had attacked the wrong man. I couldn't wait for the doors to close and drive out of the station.

•   •   •

Being an athlete, through the factory where my Mother worked, I was invited to take part in the works annual sports day. It was a very good day and I took part in just about everything and managed to come first in most sports for Ladies. By early evening the activities came to a close and the best sportsman and sportswoman were voted. I won the sportswoman cup and a friend of my Mothers won the Sportsman cup. After the presentations were done and dusted, there was a bar-b-que followed by a live band and dancing in a marquee. Mum didn't wish to stay for the evening, but me being the Sportswoman of the day I was invited to stay for the evening dance. I was only 16 at the time and Mum was not happy to leave me there alone without a chaperone. Her work mate was Sportsman of the day and he offered to look after me and to also see that I got home safely at the end of the evening. His wife was not a very friendly woman and she too did not wish to stay for the evenings frivolities. In hindsight I think they had had some sort of argument. The two women left together leaving me to enjoy my accolade with Sportsman of the day a very good looking, bronzed muscular man of 32. We spent the evening naturally together, laughing, talking and dancing. By the end of the nights' fun it was time to go home, but, it was now much later than Mum had allowed me to be out without her. The man in question told me not to worry; he would make sure that I got home safely. We had missed the last bus and I was somewhat disturbed as to how I would get back to Balham. But, he is twice my age and I knew I could trust him. Well…I thought I could and we all know what thought did don't we? Walking slowly together across the fields to get to a taxi rank, I was suddenly thrown to the ground and jumped on. We always ask such stupid questions at times like this. I actually said, "What are you doing?" What a waste of time you know damn well what he is doing and he did. I put up a very strong fight but after all he was twice my size and full of muscles. He wasn't completely successful. I had been terrified. Here was a married man, a workmate of my Mum with whom she had left me with and trusted him to look after me. Some people you can't trust. One saving grace was what my Mother had taught me from a very early age, always keep your hand on your ha'penny and if you can get your legs doubly crossed, rape is impossible. She was right. I never told my Mother what had happened. This man followed me for weeks, always stalking me and standing on every street corner waiting for me, until I asked the boys in my sports club to see him off. After that he fortunately disappeared.

After reading these items, I bet you're glad you didn't live in Balham in those days.

Chapter Eight
LOOKING ON THE BRIGHTER SIDE OF LIFE.

On a happier note, for my sister and me, Saturday morning was a treat. We would go on the tram to Tooting Market and buy 6 penny worth of crab's legs and also watch the fishmonger chop the writhing eels into little pieces. On getting home we would make our way to the scullery, get the coal hammer from the cellar and smash the crab's legs on the wooden draining board to be able to extract the juicy meat. Wonderful! To this day crab's legs still excite me just the same.

Having now left school I applied for my first real job. This was in Harrods in the children's wear department ages 2 to 7. (See book 1 for further details) The time spent there was a very good learning curve. It taught me how to behave slightly better than I had been used to, how to speak the Queen's language better and most important, people skills. The only slight problem I encountered was my clothing. The ruling in the days of Sir Richard Burbridge was that all female staff would wear black clothing of which I had none and could not afford to buy new. So I was learning the hard way, make do with what you have. I bought some Dylon dyes and changed the colour of some of my outfits overnight to the obligatory black. The clothes needed quite a bit of darning, so Aunty Minnie next door once again came in very handy.

During my time in Harrods I was also taught window dressing and display. This caused another little problem. Every time I bent down to arrange the display, my stockings would hole and ladder. I obviously had to buy a new pair during working hours. Even with a staff discount, an ordinary pair of nylons cost me one week's wages, so I politely suggested to my Buyer that as the work I was doing was for Harrods, Sir Richard should pay for the nylons. Much to my surprise I won, but, I was asked to be more careful in future. Even people who have money are still very tight fisted. Perhaps that is why they have money. There are many stories in book 1 entitled "Chance of a Lifetime" about my experiences at Harrods.

As I grew older I gradually began to know my Father and both my sister and I had very memorable walking holidays with him around Norfolk and his birthplace of Tadcaster in Yorkshire. There will always be a certain part of my body that will long remember one visit to Tadcaster. Dad bought a tandem and fitted to it a small petrol engine, which we called a "Pop Pop", purely because that's the noise it made. On the designated day of departure we left his house in Acton, West London, very early in the morning, to be precise 5.30.a.m. We set off at a good pace feeling happy but hungry. The idea to leave early was to avoid rush hour traffic and have an early starter breakfast at a Little Chef. My memory still tells me that was one of the best breakfasts I have ever had. Fully satiated we saddled up and began the very long ride to Tadcaster. After many hours in the saddle we stopped at a bikers' road side café for lunch. Unfortunately it was now pouring with rain and to say that we are both cold and very wet puts in mildly. I went into the Ladies for two reasons, and the second one was to take off some of my clothes, literally wring them out and put them back on again. Your flesh becomes very cold and clammy and I just longed to be warm. But.... not to be downhearted we ate a good lunch, kitted ourselves out again in all the wet gear, saddled up, started the little POP...POP and with a heavy weight of wet clothes pedalled off into the rain storm. After cycling for 15 hours in the rain, a certain part of my body is not feeling very good and I can no longer remain in the saddle as I am also falling asleep whilst pedalling.

Having arrived at Grantham railway station, we bought three tickets for Tadcaster one each for Dad and me and one for the tandem. On arriving at our destination we unloaded the bike and our luggage, started the motor and began the final part of the journey. At last it had left off raining and the final stage of the journey was a little better, until we met the cobbled streets leading into Tadcaster. I could no longer sit on the saddle and had to peddle standing up, the pain was, how you say, "rather uncomfortable". We finally arrived at Grannies at about 10.00 p.m. happy, hungry, tired and sore. It was 5 days before I could sit down on anything other than a rubber ring. I took the train back to Balham, threatening never again to do something that stupid.

•   •   •

After working my way through numerous boy friends, I finally accepted a proposal of marriage and in September of 1958, the knot was tied. My husband was an ironmonger, running a small shop for his Mother. His Father had died many years previously leaving his Mum to run the shop. Her health was deteriorating rapidly so that is when we took over the day to day running of the shops.
Later after her unfortunate death, my husband and I now owned the shops and we added more making a final total of 7. This consisted of Hardware, D.I.Y. Builders yard, an Interflora Florist, Lawn Mower engineering workshop and our own Wholesale Company. As you can see we were kept

fairly busy. After training hard for a few years I became a professional lady Ironmonger and also a professional Interflora Florist.

This next story I call it "Have a nice day". Through our Interflora services, I sent a birthday bouquet from a client in England, who was a Texan, to his daughter in America. The transaction was dealt with over the telephone, where he paid by credit card. The goods were duly delivered on the correct day, but, were definitely below Interflora standards. My client phoned me a few days later to tell me in no uncertain terms just what he thought of the delivered bouquet and that he had not got his monies worth. Before I could assure him that this would definitely be dealt with he was called away on business without leaving me his number in England. Not wishing to have an unhappy customer I sent a telex from Interflora headquarters to the executing florist in USA to find out the facts. Just 24 hours later my telex was returned and the overseas florist assured me that she had apologised to the customer and replaced the goods. She had also sent a complimentary bouquet to help ease the disappointment. Now, this left the "birthday girl" and the florist satisfied but not me or my customer. I wrote to the daughter in USA extending my personal apologies and best wishes for her birthday and hoped that her initial disappointment at the quality of the flowers had not spoilt her celebrations. At this time I also pointed out that I had been unable to contact her father to explain to him the actions I had undertaken or to extend to him personally my apologies and hoped that she would convey this message to her father for me. For weeks I heard nothing, until one morning at about mid-day, someone with a very strong Texan drawl, phoning from Texas was asking for me by name. This was my original client who wished to thank me for all the time, effort, trouble and kindness I had shown to both his daughter and him and remarked that I deserved to have a successful business. I was taken aback, returned the thanks and said that I hoped we would continue to do business together for many years to come. His final remark was thus, "Have a nice day Ann" and then hung up. As an Interflora Florist we delivered to 135 countries including Moscow. The only place to my knowledge where Interflora doesn't operate is the Antarctic..........but then only penguins go there.

The second difficult Interflora delivery was even more bizarre. It was Valentines Day and the gentleman customer requested one red rose to be delivered to the airport in Jersey. Sounds easy. But it wasn't. His girl friend was arriving on a specific flight from England to Jersey on Valentines Day and the request was thus. As she walked off the plane the red rose was to be handed to his girl friend with a proposal of marriage. Isn't life romantic sometimes? It makes you want to shed some quiet tears. After many phone calls to Jersey and the airport staff, I finally managed to comply with his request. She accepted his proposal and after they were married they both came into my shop to say "Thank you".

•　　　　　•　　　　　•

I then developed this tremendous urge to have children so on the

10th August 1960 our first son Ian was born in Epsom General Hospital weighing in at 6lbs 10ozs. 18 months later the second son Keith was born at home weighing in at 5lbs 6ozs. I then made a momentous decision. Two children will be enough. I was never very sure who our sons inherited their mischievous behaviour from. Most of the family said that it could only be from me. When the boys were very young, due to their excitable nature and unruly behaviour, I suffered a nervous breakdown and had tried to take an overdose as I couldn't stand the trauma anymore. For 6 weeks the boys were taken away from me to a day centre to allow me some quality time and to try to gain some control in my life. The Doctors said that I had two very lively children who would go far. Once or twice I added a suggestion as to how far, but it was not allowed. I would take them every morning after breakfast to the Day Centre where they would remain until I collected them at 6.00.p.m take them home, give them their tea and a bath, put them to bed, read a story and then relax until the following day. By the end of the 6 weeks I had recovered. I then told myself that no person would ever again rule my life, that I would be strong and deal with any problems that would arise. Like all siblings, there was rivalry and fighting, plus that well known saying, "It wasn't me Mum it was him".Mischief seemed to be their middle names. Whatever one son didn't think of, the other one did. I'm now going to embarrass the boys and put in print some of their antics. They filled every key hole in our bungalow with Polyfilla, decorated the hall with red Tuxan shoe polish and placed matchsticks in the power sockets, just to see what would happen. Their ingenuity seemed to have no boundaries.

The youngest son climbed a step ladder that was against the fence at the bottom of the garden, tripped and fell through the greenhouse roof. I at the time, was in the kitchen doing what Mums do, peeling spuds for lunch when I heard the breaking sound of glass. I looked through the kitchen window to see my son lying on the floor inside the greenhouse with shards of glass hanging precariously around his neck. I screamed at him to keep still as I belted down the garden path barefooted. I climbed inside the greenhouse and rescued him alive and well. He received no cuts at all as his nappy had protected his nether regions and his long trousers the rest of his body. I was a different kettle of fish, wearing no shoes and treading on broken glass to rescue him caused me, as you might say, some cuts to my feet. I am being modest here. Oh well we are both still very much alive.

Some children seem to court disaster and mine are no exception. There are many times throughout their young lives that I thought, this could be their last adventure, but fortunately I was wrong, they are both still very much alive and always up for anything. Must be some characteristic inherited from their Mother!! One particular day is hard to forget. I collected some of their school friends and took them all to Surbiton Lagoon for a day swimming and playing games. I had taken a picnic for us all, 7 in total. After many hours of fun in the open air pool and the fountain we sat on a rug, suitably supplied by me and ate heartily of the picnic. Finally when it became time to go home we all disappeared to our respective changing rooms. On locating my locker I discovered that it was open and there were

73

none of my clothes to be seen. I went to the reception desk to report this matter but nothing seemed to solve the problem. Picture the scene, I am now left with 7 small boys I am dressed only in a bikini and I am driving them all home. At one particularly busy roundabout there was a policeman on duty as the lights had failed. He stopped me and questioned me as to my motives for driving half naked accompanied by 7 small boys. You can probably guess what he thought, but he wasn't right. Eventually the boys convinced him that they were O.K. and after lots of horn honking from passers by we were allowed to go on our way. 2 weeks later my clothes were found.

One beautiful afternoon my Mother arrived to see the two grand children, who were playing happily in the back garden. So we came indoors for a well earned cuppa. After a while we could hear what sounded like the ripple of water. On going into the hall of my bungalow I am suddenly ankle deep in water, which I finally discovered was coming from the cistern. I quickly ran in there and tied up the valve with a piece of wood and string to stop the flow. I then proceeded into the garden to check the overflow pipe to see why this hadn't worked. The pipe was full of play doh, pencils and clothes pegs, which the kids had hidden as they thought, in a safe place. But of course being a lady plumber I was quite able to put this matter right, and then spent the entire afternoon mopping. Aren't kids great, sometimes? The boys were now growing rapidly and went to the local junior school until the age of 11, whereupon they both attended the local comprehensive school and both "passed out", with flying colours. Perhaps when I am old and decrepit they will be able to support me in the manner to which I have now become accustomed. Who knows? A girl can dream.

My Husband and I being in business locally were very involved with the Chamber of Commerce. My Husband was a Rotarian and I an Inner Wheel Member. Raising money for our local people less fortunate than ourselves has always been uppermost in my mind and to this end my brain cells started grinding away to think of a unique way to not only raise money but for everyone to have fun doing it. I involved all our local shopkeepers and staff in a BIKEATHON. Each shop outlet had to dress all the staff in costume of their choice. Anything on wheels was allowed. We had unicyclists, 2 wheelers 3 wheelers, 4 wheelers, roller skates, prams and pushchairs. The plan was thus: to all gather together on the village green for instruction and safety procedures. The Mayor would start the ride by waving a large pink feather duster. The route was circular around the village into Epsom and back again, with stations en route for medical help and drinks. The maximum distance to cover was 4 circuits of 5 miles each, with no cheating. On the way people were giving us money for our cause, and sometimes we even stopped and visited the local pubs to beg for more money. The day was a Sunday so the roads were not too busy but the pubs were full. You see some of us take the time to make a note of these devious plans. It was a good fun day, lots of giggles, some blisters, some sore sit me downs, everyone in costume of some sort plus money raised for some of our less fortunate neighbours. All in all the day was a great success. Life at this time for us both was fairly hectic. I was secretary to the Chamber of Commerce, including writing articles for the local papers. My Husband was chairman of the Rotary club at the same time as I was President of my Inner Wheel Club. We only used to meet once a week going upstairs to bed, life was so busy, but fun. During my time as President of Ewell Inner Wheel, I had the frightening honour to speak at the Blackpool Conference to over 5,000 women. I had to put forward a resolution asking all members to vote against illegal Sunday Trading and to stop the introduction of legal Sunday trading. This I believe has to be 1972 or thereabouts. You can tell that I made no inroads into this subject. My talk had to last exactly 3 minutes. I sat up half the night before, with my friends from Inner Wheel, timing very carefully the 3 minutes allotted time. On the day of my talk I was called for and made a very nervous walk to the platform and put my notes on the lectern. On the top of this lectern were 3 lights. One green, one orange and one red. When the green light came on I started to speak slowly and clearly. After one and a half minutes the amber light came on reminding me that I only had another one and a half minutes before the red light would come on and the microphone cut off. If I had not finished speaking no one could hear me. Fortunately I had rehearsed very well and I finished 30 seconds before the cut off. Phew.

If my husband and I were lucky we could get away from our businesses sometimes for a well earned holiday. We booked a trip to Spain, with our two sons. We were travelling in a very old Ford utility truck, black in colour so we named her "Black Bertha". We drove down to Portsmouth where we picked up a boat to take us to Santander. This was a 36 hour mini cruise. The weather was not too rough until we got to the Bay of Biscay. Perhaps rough is not the correct description, rolling would describe it more accurately. This is where I decided to take part in clay pigeon shooting. After a very brief lesson on what to do, I yelled out "Pull". As I fired off the double barrelled shotgun the recoil was stronger than I had expected and it threw me over backwards into the arms of my tutor who happened to be a rather young good looking Spaniard. For a brief moment I didn't notice the pain, but all too soon I was very aware of this sharp pain in my right shoulder. The butt of the rifle had recoiled into my bra strap and made a wonderful bruise the exact shape of the buckle. I felt very proud of this. Not that I could show it to anyone. The up side of this adventure was that I hit the corner of no less than 5 clay pigeon. So you see it was not all in vain. My sons were sort of proud of their Mum.

The rest of the holiday was good fun, good food, and lots of sunshine, swimming and playing on the sandy beaches with the family, doing what families do on holiday. I'm not sure why things seem to go wrong with me when on holiday. My family of 4 and my friends' family of 4 took the same big black Ford utility truck on a camping holiday to France. We consisted of 4 young boys and 4 adults out for some more adventures. All 4 adults were drivers and so we took it in turns at the wheel to give each of us a break from driving on the WRONG side of the road in a very heavily laden truck with no air conditioning. Our air conditioning was much more basic we could slide open both of the front doors and lock them back, which gave us some slight draught and ventilation. After a lunch stop it was my turn at the wheel. So with a happy heart we all clambered aboard, I took to the wheel and off we sped further into France. We are now somewhere in the countryside looking for our next port of call. I am driving up a bit of a steep hill and as you can imagine the truck was struggling. On reaching the top of the hill there was a level crossing, our Black Bertha was not happy. So being the skilled driver I thought I was I shifted from 2nd gear into 1st. In the middle of the crossing the engine coughed, spluttered and final gave up the ghost. Can you imagine how I am feeling? The 4 boys are trapped in the back of the van with no easy quick escape route. I slammed on the brakes, quickly ran to the back of the truck, opened the door, dragged the boys out and told them to run away as fast as they could. We strong adults then released the brakes and began to try to push this big truck to safety, all the while keeping a very careful eye on the railway lines in both directions. After what seemed an eternity the truck finally gave in and we managed to push it to safety. I think you could have heard our sigh of relief back in England. After collecting our thoughts of what might have been, the next task was to see if the clever men folk could determine what had caused this malfunction and near disaster. Upon closer inspection one of the men noticed that the gear stick, which in those days was on the steering wheel, was still in 3rd gear. Neutral was found and the ignition key turned, and you've guessed it, the engine sprang into life. These old Ford Utility trucks, as I said had the gear stick on the steering wheel, just 1st, 2nd, 3rd and a reverse. 1st and 3rd happened to be very near in proximity to each other. In my moment of panic I had shifted to 3rd not 1st which is why it stalled. It has taken me many years to live that one down. On arrival at the next town, we asked one of the locals as to how often there was a train going across the level crossing. His reply was great "There is no need for you to worry there is only one train a week". Knowing my luck I could have chosen the wrong day of the week. After some suitable beverages to settle our nerves, we set off again with a different person at the controls. I couldn't think why, as I had not done my full stint.

We are now in need of some petrol, so that was our next task to find a garage. Our luck had started to change as after a very short time we came across a garage and started to fill up. One small problem we are having is that we seem to be unable to find the location of our next camp site called La Dolce Vita. At the next petrol pump to us was a very French looking gentleman doing the same as us, so we decided to ask him the way. My friends all voted that it should be me to ask the question as my French was better than theirs. I approached the gentleman and said, "Bonjour Monsieur, s'il vous plait, ou est La Dolce Vita campsite?" He gave me a strange look and then replied in his very best Scottish accent. "Och aye I dunno ken my sen, I am on holiday here from Edinburgh". (Sorry about the Scottish words, but you Scots out there can put them right) Whilst everyone in the garage forecourt is laughing at this piece of humour I quickly got back in the van and pulled away on the wrong side of the road. I did wonder why I was being heavily beeped. We all suddenly realised my error and they all screamed out right hand down, which as you can imagine I did in rather a hurry. We are now driving somewhere in France looking for this elusive campsite where we hope to spend the night. Whilst driving through country lanes we spotted a very French looking farmer, dressed as you would expect a French farmer to look, navy dungarees and the obligatory beret at a jaunty angle. He was walking beside his farm cart loaded with hay and pulled by a rather large horse. What a fabulous scene depicting rural France. We all decided that this would be the person to ask for our directions. Once again I was nominated as the better French speaking person to approach this farmer. I carefully worked out my French and approached the farmer. He dutifully stopped his horse and I said, "Excuse moi, ou est La Dolce Vita campsite?" I paused and waited for his reply, "Nicht sprachen Francais". Amidst howls of laughter and lots of the only words I knew in German we bade him farewell, Aufwiedersehen.

We have all now decided that to find this campsite would be out of the question and our holiday might come to an end before we found anyone in France who could speak French or alternatively anyone who had ever heard of this particular site. We opened our maps and found another site easier to find, arrived, pitched a tent and settled in for the night, weary but happy. When morning broke, the sun was shining, the camp site in the daytime looked good, but as we were late arriving last night we had little or no food for breakfast. We drove off into a small town to buy whatever we needed. Our luck was in, this very day was market day and the place was buzzing with people and some wonderful looking foods. We spied the meat stall and made our way there to buy some sausages for breakfast, not knowing that French sausages are twice the size of the English version. Once again in my best French accent I spoke to the assistant and said, "Bonjour, je desire soixante saucisson s'il vous plait". Her eyebrows rose in disbelief and she said, "Combien?" Oh dear! I had asked for 60 sausages and not 16, So we all stood there and began to count, une, deux, trios, quatre, cinq, etc until we reached 16 which is Seize. By now the entire market area is laughing at these strange English people who were trying to speak French. But not to be daunted we joined in with the fun and in the end we thought we did very well, purchasing all our requirements needed for a good meal.

Has anyone reading this piece ever eaten a large French sausage? As far as we were concerned they were impossible to cook and even after 1 hour on the fire they still looked and tasted raw. We finally gave up trying and went out to eat instead. These 16 sausages met an untimely departure from this world, but, much to the joy of all concerned. The rest of our holiday was to us almost normal. But wait a mo' another story has just sprung into my memory. We were now driving along a country road somewhere in France, my Husband was at the wheel and my girl friend and I were at the rear of the van trying to hold everything in place each time the vehicle made a sharp turn. Alongside the road was an avenue of bushes and small trees which were being trimmed by a very large piece of machinery, which we obviously avoided. Once back on the straight and narrow again, upon looking out of the back window of the truck we both saw a car tyre literally rolling away down the hill. We both laughed, as you do at other people's misfortune. We then were very aware that our vehicle was making a very loud scraping noise, like metal on concrete. This was our tyre rolling off into the distance. The Y shaped piece of metal holding it in place had lost its nut and bolt and that was what we could hear scraping. We screamed at the men folk to stop so that we could run at speed back down the road to retrieve our spare wheel. Then we managed to tie everything up once again with a piece of string and a scarf. We Brits are at times so clever and full of ingenuity.

One little piece of excitement happened in Valencia up a mountain. The 4 boys went off on an adventure alone. Some time later 2 of the boys returned out of breath and quite distraught. My youngest son had fallen in the mountains and impaled the top of his leg on a large pine needle. The older boys had managed to pull him off and dragged him into the shade being looked after by one other boy whilst the others ran to us for help. The temperature was very high, so we stopped to put on our hats and some clothes to protect us from the sun. After some fairly hairy climbing we located the wounded son. Having to carry him and climb down the mountain at the same time in 90 degree heat was to say the least pushing us all very hard. On reaching safety, we all loaded ourselves into the van and began to look for a hospital. We asked the security guard of the campsite to direct us to the nearest hospital, showing him our son's leg. In no uncertain terms he told us that he did not speak English. We asked many people for help to locate a hospital, but we did not win. Suddenly whilst driving we saw this sign which said "Hospital". Pronounced as "OOPITAL" in Spanish. Frustration begins to get the better of you sometimes. This turned out to be a Nunnery with a nurse who was skilled in stitching wounds. She applied 4 clips and said keep it dry and see your Doctor on arriving in England. To cut this long story short it finally went sceptic and needed a large skin graft which took place in Roehampton Hospital. He now proudly sports a large dent in the top of his leg. The skin that covered the hole came from his bottom. Not a lot of people have skin on their legs which was once on their bum. I can honestly say that the rest of the holiday went as planned, well that was until we tried to get off the ferry when arriving back in England. The solenoid on the truck had broken and the only way to start the vehicle was to use the starting handle. Yes you heard correctly a starting handle. We could only insert this after the vehicle in front of us had moved and by the time we had the vehicle moving, all aboard were getting very impatient. Going through customs they wanted to check our vehicle for contraband and insisted that we turn off the ignition even though we tried to explain our difficulty to no avail. So we switched off whilst we were searched. Yes, we could not get it going again, it took all of us pushing to jump start this errant truck, but we finally managed and luckily made it home without too much trouble. The only thing we couldn't do was to stop for a meal.

I have all my life wanted to be a performer and although I gained a place at RADA I could not attend as Mum needed me to go to work to earn money. Being my own BOSS I could perform when I wanted to, not when perhaps an agent wanted me to, so not going to RADA had a good outcome in the end. Another fascinating exploit being involved with Inner Wheel, I wrote, produced, directed and performed in many shows for over ten years. We entertained Senior Citizen clubs, Disadvantaged people in Hospital, physically and mentally disabled children and elderly people of the Abbey Field society group. I had the time of my life for those 10 years. Being able to make people laugh or sometimes just smile is one of the most rewarding things that anyone can do. I would sometimes perform one of Pam Ayres poems, The Battery Hen, dressed as a chicken and cluck and lay pretend eggs into a bucket at the end of each verse, whilst the audience laughed their heads off. You see I told you I was different. Being in business locally and very involved with the Chamber of Commerce, our local shopping centre needed an advertising boost and to help in this end I was asked to help with the advertising. We have a local spring and the young ducklings would waddle through our village so the advertising symbol was a Duck.

I converted my chicken costume into a duck costume and rode in a crane bucket over the spring. This too made the local papers.

My adventures still had not come to an end. Read on, there's more.

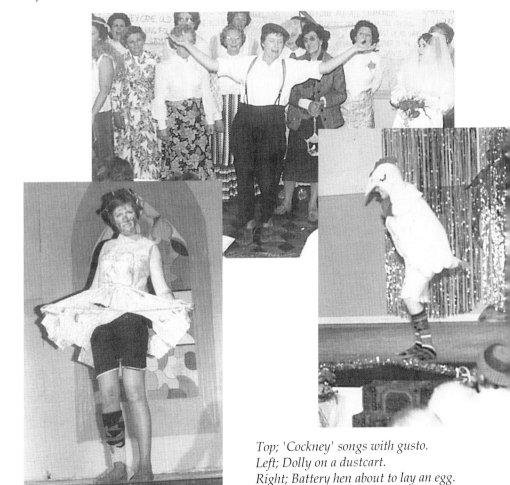

Top; 'Cockney' songs with gusto.
Left; Dolly on a dustcart.
Right; Battery hen about to lay an egg.

Chapter Nine
YET MORE OF "UVER FINGS WOT I 'AVE DUN"

Due to the fact that I had worked with physically disabled adults for quite some time, my presence was known.

I was telephoned by an organisation, based in Balham, who helped parents of disabled youngsters. This particular family was having some difficulty with their Spina Bifida adult son and the parents were in desperate need of a break. A meeting with the family, the son and me was arranged to firstly see if we could get on with each other and secondly to ask me if I would take this young man to Tenerife for a holiday with all expenses paid. After some quite lengthy discussions, I gave my consent and so did the young man. All the plans were made and the departure date got nearer and nearer.

Doubt on my behalf began to creep in rather rapidly. What could I do I had said yes and accepted this tremendous responsibility. Some things went well and others...............well, I cannot go into details as I need to preserve some privacy. Sometimes tempers were flared and on other occasions they were better. My saving grace was due to the fact that this Hotel caters for disabled people so I was not alone, and quickly made friends with all the other residents.

Do you remember that I have often said that strange things happen to me? Here we go again. One sunny afternoon sitting around the pool, swatting the cockroaches and helping the wheelchair users to play chess, a disabled young man, who by the way was an ex jockey from Epsom Derby stables, asked me if I would give him a shave as his hands were not functional and he wanted to look good for the evening. So being the carer that I was and feeling sorry for this young man I dutifully offered my services. On entering his room I got all the gear ready to give him a wet shave. To enable me to do this I am now sitting in front of this man in his wheelchair with my legs around his to enable me to get close to his chin. I am no more than 2 minutes into the shave when his hands suddenly appear to not be as dysfunctional as they were a few minutes ago. They were now wandering in places that normally only mine go when I am having a shower. What shall I do? Shall I cut his throat with the razor, slap his face or run screaming from his room. I threw his razor down, slapped his face and quickly left his room. My young man had seen what happened and came to my rescue. Four other male wheelchair users banded together and told this half shaven man what they thought of him. For the rest of the week, if this person came anywhere near me all the wheelchair users would block him off, whilst fully protecting me. I felt very important and very grateful to all these other lovely young men for looking after me.The rest of the week went without a hitch and although I enjoyed spending time with a very lively group of disabled folk, I swear there are some things that I will never do again, w e l l probably not for a long time any way.

•   •   •

During my flying days there were many adventures, some of which I can talk about. I have sustained a brake failure on landing and could not stop on the runway. My passenger was quite excited. I then managed to get onto the escape route and steered from side to side to get enough friction to slow the aircraft. I could see the perimeter fence getting very near, but with a lot of luck and a small amount of skill I managed to stop the aircraft. The fire crew were immediately alongside me and offered to give me a fireman's lift, which I'm sorry to say I declined their very friendly offer. It was at this point that I started to hyperventilate due to shock and one of the firemen started to thump my chest and said "Big breaths". I can't help it, but humour seemed to take over and I replied, "Yeth, and I'm only thixteen". The day ended in laughter which as we all know, is good for you. I have flown into a flock of birds on take off from Biggin Hill; luckily they went left as I flew right.

I have also had my rudder drop off as I landed. I think it was the string that broke. I was very glad it broke on the ground and not in the air.

I have also had my alternator go down over the White Cliffs of Dover. This feeds your batteries and I had no idea how much flying time I had left before it failed me. All the instruments suddenly read zero and I had no radios and could not speak to my passenger. Keeping the panic mode under control was quite difficult not to let my friend see how much I was worried. I knew I had plenty of fuel as I had filled up to the tabs before take off. That's one worry less to deal with. I then made my way back to Biggin Hill keeping fields underneath me in case I needed to make an emergency landing. As I approached Biggin Hill my next concern reared its ugly head. How do I ask for permission to come in and land? From somewhere in the back of my mind I remembered seeing a war film where the returning pilot had the same problem so I did as he had done, I over flew the control tower and waggled my wings. I am told that this informed them that I could fly but could not communicate with them. My eyes are now out on organ stops looking for other aircraft in the vicinity. I suddenly noticed a small plane which had been in the circuit and he suddenly started to orbit away from the runway. This told me that the tower had informed all pilots that they

81

had an emergency and I was given priority to come in and land. The next ugly problem reared its head; I have no electricity, no flaps, no air speed and no height indicator. Oooer. You're on yer own Annie. Sweating profusely I came in to land and did a goodun' so the boys at the club told me. I do now know what it's like to land by the seat of your pants. I don't recommend it, but it works. I was even congratulated by the tower for the manoeuvre I had performed with the waving wings, it was exactly correct. So you see watching old war time movies can sometimes save your life.

I have suffered Air Rage. I was given permission to come in and land number 1, which I confirmed. I am on final approach to land when a twin engine aircraft overtook me and landed in front of me exactly in the space that I was about to put down in. I quickly pulled up my flaps, applied full power, veered to the left and screamed at the control tower, "I'm going around, I'll say it again, I'm going around". He managed to have his license revoked for a few months I'm glad to say. My next landing was good and luckily I was the only one landing at the same time on this occasion. So you see, flying can be quite fun.

A group of intrepid flyers, I amongst them had been invited to have a corporate day out in Bruntingthorpe in Leicester. This was to be a treat by the gentleman who owns Caterham kit cars. His wife passed her P.P.L the day before me and so her husband decided to spoil a number of us who had also passed their test at about the same time. We were twelve in number. On the day of departure the weather was everything we desired. After completing our final flight checks, headings and weather we all lined up on the runway, taking off in sequence. We had decided to fly in formation so once airborne this was achieved. This flight for me was a little frightening as I had never flown this far before or landed at this strange airfield. But we pilots are made of brave stuff somewhere underneath our shaky exterior. The flight was uneventful and we arrived on time in Bruntingthorpe and all of us landed safely, I am proud to confess. We were greeted by our mentors and taken to a meeting room to be advised of the next step and then divided into three teams ready for our car racing experience. I was very proudly put into the Beneton Team. Each team member had to drive three different cars not only being timed but marked on skill and proficiency. The first car test was to drive a 3 litre Mercedes off road, through rivers, climb very steep soggy hills and manage to come down the other side in one piece.

To put the off side wheel on a high bank at an angle of 30 degrees, and drive like this for 3 minutes without toppling over. The next step was to drive slalom like between bamboo canes, trying not to knock any of them down. If you were careless enough to even touch a bamboo pole this was another point lost. Modesty here will not let me divulge just how many times I SLIGHTLY moved out of position. Suffice it to say, that the course had to be rebuilt before the next contestant could perform. The next exciting event was to drive a Caterham kit car Lotus seven around a race track at speed. We were taken once with a racing driver to show us the marked route and then you were on your own. I am now sitting very low down in this very fast racing car with the engine revving, the sun shining and my heart pounding.

The stop watch is set at ready, 5 litres of water are poured under the front wheels to make a screech sound as I put the car into 1st gear, release the brakes and I am off. I reached speeds of 120 miles per hour and still only managed to get into 3rd gear. It was so exciting and I could get some idea of what the professional racing drivers could feel. The last test and the final car was a 3 and a half litre Mercedes coupé with out riders controlled by computers, fixed to all four wheels to simulate different weather conditions, from flood water, ice and grease. At this time you are not alone in the car as the computer needs to be operated and you are taught how to deal with these various problems at speed. I have learnt how to aqua plane, how to control a skid on ice and finally how to make a last minute change of direction at a given speed.
The course was set with 3 cones thus.

A   A   A

The next task was to drive at a given speed of 70 miles an hour aiming for the centre cone. At the last minute the instructor would scream left or right and you had to follow his instruction without hitting any of the cones. After completing all the tests we were then treated to lunch after which the score board came out. We thought we had done quite well, but our marks did not reflect this. The racing drivers said we might be very good pilots, but don't give up your day jobs to try to become a racing driver. Cheeky blokes. We felt very clever, we could fly but they couldn't, they could race and we couldn't so we felt it was a draw. So thanks go to all my old flying friends for a smashing day out. So after saying our thanks and farewells we donned our Biggles flying hats and took to the skies to aim for Biggin Hill and normality.
I have a lot to thank Caterham Kit Cars for.
        My second day out with them was at Brooklands where a group of my flying companions raced the kit cars around the circuit. This was yet another memorable day of speed. WOW!!! Adventure has always been my motto and I have shared this over the years with my sister. This next expedition is definitely in the adventure mode. Another group of my flying mates had arranged to fly to Plymouth via Exeter for the weekend where we will go tall ship sailing. This large fully rigged ship is used for disadvantaged youngsters to gain experience in life. They live, sleep and eat on board for 2 weeks at a time. Their living conditions are quite rough, reminiscent of the days of Captain Bligh. My sister had asked if she could accompany me for the weekend and very happy about this I agreed. I was flying a single engine 4 seater Grumman Cheetah. I did take another pilot with me as I did not have an instrument rating and the weather south west in England can be a bit unpredictable to say the least. My sister in the back seat was the in flight caterer. She supplied the sarnis and the coffee. I told her not to drink too much as there are no toilets on board a small aircraft. For the majority of the flight the weather was perfect, but like all English weather it changed quite suddenly. Around Exeter the visibility became zero, so it was a good job I had another pilot on board who had to take over. On approaching Plymouth airport we were told to orbit as the airfield

was exceptionally busy. We started at 4,000 feet and orbited for 20 minutes each of us taking it in turns to go the other way to stop us getting dizzy. This happened at every 1000 foot drop, until finally after 45 minutes orbiting (that means going in ever decreasing circles) we were given permission to land. The visibility is still zero. So my friend is flying and I'm calling his height and speed and telling him that I do not have the runway on visual

Above;
Ready for the off to Plymouth.

Right;
An overcast sky couldn't
dampen the enthusiasm of all
on board.

yet. Suddenly at 600 feet I yelled "Runway on visual, dead ahead". He said "O.K, you can take over now and land". I grabbed the controls and came in to make a good safe landing, much to the relief of my sister whose knuckles had been white for some time. We spent a wonderful day and a half on a sailing ship, watching the youngsters run up the rigging and dealing with all the enormous sails. Lunch time came and the youngsters not only cooked but waited on us as well. The food was great. We spent one whole day sailing around the harbour of Plymouth, sharing experiences with the young crew. The next day when we were due to fly back to Biggin Hill the fog had not cleared so we had to wait until about 12 noon before the visibility was good enough to see where we were going. So after a light lunch we all decided to make our way back singly rather than in formation. I chose to fly along the coast line all the way from Plymouth, just meandering until I came to Brighton marina where I turned left and made my way to Biggin Hill airfield. What a wonderful experience that weekend had been.

A married couple, friends of mine, were both celebrating their 60th birthdays within a day or two of each other. The husband had asked me secretly if I could take them both for a flight. His wife had always wanted to fly over the white cliffs of Dover on a wing and a prayer and he could think of no better person to help her achieve this ambition.

I had to be very careful planning this flight due to the fact that both my friends were, how do you say, rather well endowed. The weight had to be carefully worked out as to who should sit where, but with some help from the boys at Biggin Hill this was soon sorted. My take off run took a little longer, as I needed more speed to get lift off. My friends didn't know that I was a bit worried I'm glad to say, but with a big sigh of relief we finally became airborne and on our way to Dover and the White cliffs. The weather was beautiful and sunny which made the cliffs look fantastic. On reaching the coast, I flew just a short way out to sea so that we could come in on a wing and a prayer, which we did whilst singing the Dam buster theme tune. It was not only for my friends a wonderful day but also for me to be able to share this experience with them. To be honest we did all have a few tears of emotion. My next little bit of concern was approaching to land. With all the extra weight on board I knew that I would hit the dirt quicker than usual. With all flaps down and taking a longer run at it we finally touched down and in one piece. No one ever did this for MY birthday and somehow just getting a birthday card would never be the same.

I have had many other exciting expeditions whilst flying and a number of them are related in book 1 "Chance or a Lifetime". One day I was taking part in yet another lesson with my instructor. We were at the end of the runway and had been given permission for take off. On this day, the wind was not in a good direction so I had to use the small bumpy runway. I applied full power and began my take off run, just as I reached lift off speed a flock of birds took to the skies in front of my plane. I yelled at the instructor for help whereupon he immediately ducked down and covered his face and told me, "Keep flying there is a good chance they will all miss us". I'm very pleased to say, they did. Phew!! The second episode was just as exciting. Another of my friends asked to go flying with me so that we could over fly his back garden and wave to his wife who had placed a sheet on the lawn to enable me to locate the garden. I checked the weather, did all my flight checks and all looked good. Take off was fine and the flight was good, we even saw the sheet on the lawn and I did what all good pilots do, I waved the aircraft wings to let his wife know that we were overhead. What a wonderful sight! Whilst flying along the south coast of England, I looked to my right to see two large twisters over Lewes in West Sussex. I knew that I had to get back to Biggin Hill rather rapidly to avoid this phenomenon. So quickly in fact my friend never had time to photograph the twisters. Later at home that evening we were all watching the news, and as you have guessed the story of the twisters made headlines as there had been substantial damage to the area. The newscaster asked anyone who had seen them and taken a picture, the B.B.C. would be grateful to have copies. Sometimes not everything in your life works out right does it?

I don't suppose for one minute that I am the only person on the planet who has taken part in a hot air balloon ride, but I bet not everyone has had the same experience as me, well I hope not, otherwise this story will be of no interest. The flight was booked but it was some time before the event could take place due to that funny thing called weather. Finally one late afternoon my sister and I arrived in this field somewhere in Paddock Wood to prepare for this flight. Unfortunately the wind was still a little too strong so we had to wait until much later when it finally reached a level that was acceptable to the pilot. The inflating of the balloon was quite a feat for all taking part. It isn't until you see one of these at close quarters that

Over the back garden of Mohamed-el Fayad.
He was not very happy, but we told him we must go where the wind takes us.

you realise just how big they are. There were at least 20 people taking part in the inflation process, even to the more intrepid amongst us who were asked to crawl inside the balloon to help with this momentous task. The basket was then tipped onto its side whilst attached to the balloon and the passengers were instructed as to how to climb aboard. This was a Virgin balloon which had 4 compartments plus the centre one for the pilot. Into each compartment climbed three intrepid travellers. As the balloon became bigger the basket finally tipped up the correct way and on the given command all the ropes were released and we slowly but surely began to rise. What a strange but wonderful experience to fly silently over beautiful English countryside. We did fly over a famous persons back garden who was not too pleased, but we shouted down to him, "We must go where the wind takes us, sorry". I enjoyed every moment of this wonderful trip. The only down side was that it was coming to an end.

The pilot informed us how to prepare for landing as he approached a suitable field. We are all squatting down in crash positions in our own little compartment waiting for the thump, when the pilot yells out that the wind has changed direction and tells us that we can't land here so please all stand up. Being very obedient people we all did as instructed. The pilot is now looking for another suitable landing field. After about 15 minutes he tells us that he has a suitable field in sight, all please adopt landing positions. As you can imagine now we are all highly skilled at squatting on command. We are now slowly descending and all is looking good. We are no more than 2 feet from the ground when suddenly out from under a group of trees run 6 very large horned bulls coming straight for our balloon. The pilot yells out, "Everyone stand, landing aborted". You know how you can think you're helping to gain height when it is imperative that you do, so we all did it, by pretending to jump up to gain height. Of course it didn't work, but we felt that it did. I asked the pilot, "Is this basket waterproof as I can see the Thames ahead getting nearer and nearer?" Modesty does not permit me to repeat his reply. By now night time is falling quite quickly and we still haven't found anywhere to land and our pick up vehicle cannot find us. Eventually doing what all good pilots do, he found a landing site in a field with weeds about 5 feet high and plenty of stinging nettles. So once again we all adopted the landing pose and waited once again for the thump, which eventually came as a shock to the system as the ground is harder than you can imagine. The basket was now down, but it was being dragged by the wind. Some of us tried to escape the basket but were told in no uncertain tones, "STAY". What we didn't know was that if we had got out, the basket would have taken off again, albeit with a few less passengers but nevertheless airborne. At last with tremendous skill and courage the pilot brought the balloon to a standstill. On his command we exited the basket, grabbed some of the ropes and helped to secure the balloon, which being very obedient we did. Having secured the balloon the next enormous task was to deflate it. This was achieved by all hands which was not only very physical but very cleverly achieved. The next problem now has reared its ugly head, the rescue vehicle still cannot find us as we are buried fairly deeply somewhere in Kent, in a field, quite some distance from a road, with a locked farm gate leading to our field. Our pilot was on his mobile to the rescue truck and some of us suggested that if the car would sound his horn we could let him know if we could hear it and perhaps lead him to us. Eureka! This worked, but as I said, the field was locked so he couldn't gain entry. He located the farmer who owned this field and related the difficulties. Permission was sought to not only unlock the gate but to get permission to gain entry. Now the time is midnight and we are all getting a bit jumpy as to know how we will be rescued. After what seemed like an eternity we heard the car arriving with the farmer to give us an extra hand. The balloon was loaded into its container; the basket was lifted onto the trailer and we now all felt ready to leave. But no, not yet. There was not enough room in the rescue car for all of us, so I and two others had to stand in the basket on the back of the trailer as we bumped across the very uneven field. Excitement like this doesn't come to everyone, you have to be a very special person "like wot I am". Having finally vacated the farmer's field we made it at last back to Paddock Wood where we had started some 6 hours previously. The time is now 2.00 a.m and we are all standing in this field drinking champagne to celebrate a rather unusual balloon flight courtesy of Virgin..

I BET YOU THOUGHT I HAD FINISHED BY NOW.

I have had the privilege to fly a 1946 pup out of Redhill aerodrome. This was quite some experience as it looked as if it was held together with bits of string, but as it was obviously very strong string I landed safely and have lived to tell the tale.

Chapter Ten
MORE ADVENTURES AROUND THE WORLD.

I have taken part in Cattle drives in Montana 2000, 2001, 2003, Wyoming 2002 Oklahoma 2004 and a Wagon Train expedition in the Teton mountains of Wyoming in 2007.
The above mentioned adventures can be read and experienced in Book 1. "Chance of a Lifetime".

In 2006 I visited Egypt, flying from Heathrow in an aeroplane named Nefertiti, to the Land of the Pharaohs. For a long time I have been fascinated with the history of this land. Our guide was a professor of Egyptology named Sharif, but we all called him Omar. On this trip I visited Cairo where the temperature was 45 degrees. HOT, I think is a good way to describe this. Next was the Cairo museum where I experienced the wonderful artefacts from the tomb of Tutankhamen. (I wonder what I will be buried with, probably the gas bill) then on to the Khan-el Khalili Bazaar, (the old bazaar in Cairo). I visited more temples than I thought existed, the Philae Temple, Abu Simbul, and the temple of Ramses the second which was moved by UNESCO when the Aswan High Dam was built. This remarkable feat took 8 years of painstaking work and it is impossible to see how this was achieved. I visited the valley of the Kings and Queens where I descended into a tomb, sailed in a Felucca down the Nile, visited the Pyramids and the Sphinx and finally a 3 day cruise on the famous Nile, where we were entertained by a belly dancer and then just to make us all feel stupid we had to try to emulate her, very badly as you can imagine. One evening during dinner on board, I needed something from my cabin. As I entered, there was a young male staff member in my room, as you can imagine I was a bit surprised and asked him what he was doing. He said, "Just turning down your bed Madam". So I happily left the room and went back to dinner.
When bed time drew near I went to my cabin, there on the bed made from my top quilt was a body, the head was made from a white towel and SHE

Me and my 'Hubble bubble' pipe.

Right-The famous Abu Simbel

Below- A Feluca on the River Nile.

was wearing my glasses and holding a book in her hand. What a wonderful surprise, now I knew what the man had been doing in my room. Every night there was something different to look forward to after dinner. The next night I had a crocodile on my bed made from the same piece of bedding, its mouth kept open with the T.V. control unit. The following night made me jump in fright, hanging from the rafters in my cabin was a monkey made from brown blankets, it was so realistic. What clever men we had the privilege to meet. Other holiday makers had things like swans or babies in their rooms, the variations seemed endless.

I expect many people have visited Egypt and experienced the same things as myself. What a magical place this is. I can't wait to go back again.

2007 PATAGONIA AND CHILE

What can one say about this fabulous land? A land of good wines, good people, wonderful scenery, waterfalls, caves, glaciers, icebergs, wild life and mountains. Some days were coach tours some days were hiking, some spent swimming and others just exploring. One particular day will live in my memory for all time. We were staying in a lodge called Lago Grey in Torres del Paine National Park. The Grey Glacier is part of the Southern Icecap which drains its icy waters into Lake Grey, named due to the colour of the melt water. The trip consisted of taking a small boat onto the lake and motor to the base of one of the glaciers. The walk to the very edge of the lake was quite unnerving, everything was so cold, so vast and the waters so still. Even the icebergs floating gracefully looked so peaceful and beautiful.

The Fitzroy and Torre Mountains.

The amount of clothing I was wearing was so much I felt that I could hardly move. Later I was to realise how important layers of clothing would prove. Having been fitted now with life jackets we all walked down a very small jetty and clambered aboard what looked like a very tiny boat compared to the size of the scenery around us. We motored for some time taking in the wonders of nature, the cold and surprisingly how far away the base of the glacier was. This glacier was receding at an alarming rate. The guide told us that in 2 years it had gone back 5 miles, which was obvious from the scaring of the mountain. We are now very near to the base of the 27ft high glacier; the engines were cut just to take in the magnitude of such a wonderful sight. Suddenly I heard what sounded like a cracking sound, and I actually said to the friend next to me,"Did you hear that?" "It sounds as if the glacier is falling apart". To my horror, a shard of ice 27 feet tall began to fall from the glacier. The Captain of the ship screamed at everyone to hold hard onto the boat rails as this could be rough. He immediately applied full power and backed away making sure that the back end, oops sorry, the stern was in line with the wave coming our way which had been caused by the impact of the ice hitting the water. This wave according to my estimate was almost 9-10 ft high. It was terrifying and dangerous. Will this tip the boat over, will we be hit by a large lump of ice or will I drown or freeze to death in the lake. Think positive Ann I told myself, the Captain must be used to this sort of thing happening. Later I found out that in the five years he had been doing this job nothing like this had happened before. You see I told you that it had something to do with my presence. The sight of all this ice and water coming our way was disconcerting to say the least. The boat rocked quite badly for some time but eventually we made it to a safe distance and we were all still alive, cold, frightened but alive. When the Captain felt we were at a safe distance he turned the boat around so that we could see just what had happened. One of the crew got a boat hook and pulled on board a large lump of the ice that had come apart from the glacier, broke it into small pieces and gave it to us in a local drink called Pisco sour. I don't drink alcohol under normal circumstances but this was not normal, it was the best drink I had ever tasted, with some very ancient pure clean ice to top it off.

Patagonia and Chile have to be experienced to take in the full magnitude of the beauty, the wild life, and the very friendly people not forgetting the remarkable Gauchos rounding up their cattle. I would love to have had a go, but there was no way I had the experience that they possessed. I have never seen such enormous and violent rapids and waterfalls. But eventually those two weeks had to come to an end.

For me, that's another two weeks of adventure completed and yet another dream realised.

Above- The collapse of a Glacier.

Right- Dormont Volcano

2008 SOUTH AFRICA.

2008 saw me make my first visit to South Africa. The world is such a small place. Two members in our group came from England almost on my doorstep. I bet this has happened to most of you reading this. This trip for me gave me very many mixed emotions. The poverty of the black population and how they are treated is still apparent. The Them and Us still prevails. Their living conditions have to be seen to be believed. The government does help them by building brick houses, but due to their culture they quickly revert back to their own ways, and the houses fall into disrepair very quickly. Our tour took us along the Garden Route and the beauty of the landscape of South Africa, seeing many wild animals from Elephants, Zebra, Wildebeest, Monkeys of all types including Baboons sitting on the road, Emus, Penguins, Llama and Deer, even a dung beetle doing what dung beetles do, they move it, but sorry to say no Lions.

Look at the Baby - AAh! (elephants)

I visited Rodden Island where Mandela was imprisoned by the South African police for 27 years. I spoke to one of the tour guides who had also been a prisoner on the island and I asked him how long he had served and what was his offence. His reply was so matter of fact, "5 years, because I planted a bomb in the Governors' Mansion, but as no one was killed my sentence was less severe". After his term of 5 years the prison was then closed for good and not before time in my honest opinion. A memorable visit was to the Cape of Good Hope which is the most South Western part of the African continent. 18' 28' 26' East and 34' 21' 25 South. Not a lot of people know that. I travelled in the cable car to the top of Table Mountain and had to stay there for a while as the wind had become very strong and it was not safe to descend. I have even sat astride a racing ostrich and have a photo to prove it.
South Africa was a memorable journey where we all were looked after very ably by SAGA. Which stands for Sex and Games for the Aged.

94

This is as far as you can go.

2009 ATHENS.

2009 happened to be a slightly more active year with no less than two adventures, enabling me to realise yet a few more dreams hidden away in the back of my mind from years ago.

Having always been interested in Greek/Roman history, I found a tour that would do just what I was looking for. My girlfriend asked me where I was going and I told her, "I'm going to Athens to study the Greek history ". She said, "Oh I have always hated history but can I come with you?" Of course I said, "Yes". Who knows, her ideas on school history might change, as nothing beats learning on the spot.

On arrival in Athens the weather was just as expected HOT, but we settled into the very good hotel and did what all good tourists do, we unpacked, surveyed the scene and went into the bar for a well earned drink. Day by day the wonders of Athens began to unfold, visiting museums, ancient ruins, temples, the Acropolis, Amphitheatres, the Parthenon and finally the city of Marathon. I even had the privilege to sing in the natural Amphitheatre and unfortunately every one could hear me without a microphone. The Greeks certainly knew how to build a theatre with nothing but natural equipment.

Having visited the ancient city of Marathon and actually climbed the hill to the original race track was a feat and a half for me. The climb took me over an hour to get to the top and I was so out of breath I could hardly take in what I saw. The race track is in a straight line not a circle as we had thought. To train the Greek soldiers for stamina, dressed in their full kit, shield and helmet they had to RUN up the hill and upon arriving at the top had to run the straight course of the track backwards and forwards for a

A Village called Marathon.

mile. If they could master this and still feel able to fight they were accepted into the legions. I then began to research the history of The Marathon. I was fascinated and very curious. Marathon is a Greek word meaning fennel. The city of Marathon has fields of fennel plants. The seeds of which are used as flavouring in foods. Why is a marathon 26.2 miles? Why is it called a marathon? Why not a long run that only crazy people do? It began in Greece in 490BC. 2,500 years ago. An army from Persia crossed the Aegean Sea and landed at Marathon city which is approx 25 miles from Athens. They had come to capture Marathon and then Athens. The Persians had 50,000 warriors. The defending army at Marathon approx 9,000 so were outnumbered 5 to 1. Phones had not been invented so the only way to communicate was by sending a messenger on horseback or a professional runner. The Greeks needed help so they sent a runner to get help. His name was Phillippides. He ran from Marathon to Sparta to ask the Spartans for help. The army at Marathon needed help at once but due to religious reasons, the Spartans would only help when the moon was full so, poor Phillippides had to run all the way back again with the bad news. The round trip was 150 miles.

When the Persians realised they outnumbered the Greeks 5 to 1 they decided to take half their army to Athens and leave the other half to conquer Marathon. What the Persians didn't know, was that they were facing a very smart Greek army and they were defeated, losing 6,400 warriors to the Greeks 192. According to legend, Philllippides took part in the battle after having run 150 miles to Sparta and back. When the battle was won, he was chosen to run the 25 miles from Marathon to Athens to tell them of the victory. He did make it, but was so exhausted after all his running and fighting that he collapsed after shouting "rejoice, we conquer!" and then he dropped down dead. It is said that he lives on through the heart of runners as a symbol of commitment, endurance and willpower. This battle changed history forever. But….. if the distance from Marathon to Athens was about 25 miles why is the marathon 26.2 miles I hear you ask?   Well I thought I did.

In 1896 when the first Olympic Games were inaugurated in Greece, as part of the heritage of Phillippides, runners ran 24.85 miles from Marathon Bridge to the Olympic stadium in Athens. But that's not 26.2 miles.

In 1908 when the Olympics were held in London, this bit is hard to believe. The Royal family wanted the finish line to be in front of their "Viewing box", so the course was lengthened to 26.2 miles. The King and Queen wanted the runners to come to them, not the other way around. In 1924 after 16 years of argument this length was established at the Olympics in Paris as the official marathon distance. And that my friends are why the Marathon is called the Marathon and why it is 26.2 miles in length.

The rest of my visit to Athens felt tame after this wonderful piece of history. I have to admit that my friend's view of history has now changed, I'm glad to say.

Builders at work on the Parthenon

2009 ICELAND.

Yet another dream about to come to fruition.

Volcanoes, glaciers, icebergs and ice caps have always held a mysterious fascination for me. What better way to live my dream than visit that wonderful island Iceland.

The tour was named "The land of ice and fire". After landing at Reykjavik airport we were all met by our guide Halldor, bundled into a small coach and after a brief tour of the island arrived at our Hotel. Even though the ice cap was some 60 miles away it was very easy to see it clearly. My description was that it looked like a cloud hovering over the horizon. This time was the land of the midnight sun, so as I had never experienced this before I sat on a bench in the sun until 10 00.p.m and finally made my way to bed. The next morning Halldor translated the news on the radio for us. Are you ready for this? It was reported at 9.00.a.m that the Mayor had caught the 1st Salmon of the year in the river in Reykjavík. Doesn't it make a change to hear good news instead of bad? Today we start the tour with a vengeance, visiting Thingvellir National Park, Gullifos Waterfall and the Geysir Geothermal Area, Thingvellir means "Parliament Plains" where the first assembly took place in the year 930. The river Oxara flows past the site and drops over a 9000 year old lava field. Geysir started spouting in the 13th century and stopped in 1916. Geysir was the first spouting spring which became known to Europeans and that's why all spouting springs are named Geysirs. The one spouting spring for the tourists is called Stokkur, roughly translated means "The Butter Churn". It spouts every 3-5 minutes up to 100feet high. I bet you can guess who got caught in this, to say that it was quite warm is a bit of an exaggeration. That day in the distance I could see Mount Hekla, Iceland's most active volcano. I could go on here for page after page, but that might bore you. If you want more take my advice visit Iceland and experience the wonders for yourself.

The Butterchurn which spouted every two minutes.

The Eurasion Tectonic Plates, the separation of two continents. The gap widens 2cm per year.

I crossed the Black Desert which is a part of the world's greatest lava field. We drove across a big sandy plain which was flooded in 1996 by glacier melt water from an eruption under Europe's greatest glacier called Vatnajokull. The next day we travelled through the uninhabited desolate part of the island which is a lava field covering 500sq km. Part of this expanse was where Neil Armstrong and his mates trained in 1968 before their moon landing. Iceland is between the Atlantic plate and the Eurasian plate and the plates under Iceland are moving apart 2 cms per year. Due to the many volcanic eruptions, Iceland will not divide into two islands in fact it is creating more land. I visited so many magnificent waterfalls, gorges, sulphur pools and climbed to walk alongside 25 active volcanoes and came back alive, even after spending one night in a wooden cabin on stilts on the flood plain. Supposing another volcano had erupted under the ice cap. If it had, I couldn't tell you my story.

Because I am now totally hooked on Iceland and want to see yet more I am going once again in 2012, this time to fly with my friend Halldor in a light aircraft over the volcanoes, the glaciers and the famous ice cap.

2010 AZORES.

The Azores for me was very energetic. I never realised exactly how much walking and climbing I had to do. Some days the walks were so difficult I was advised not to take part. In all I visited 6 of the volcanic islands, some by ferry and some by a light aircraft. Namely, Sao Miguel, Terciera, Velas, Madalena, Horta and Pico. The flight in the light aircraft for me made my visit worthwhile. The vineyards take up a lot of space on the islands. Once you have tasted just a few you suddenly feel more capable of participating in the climbs. To take a rest from walking and climbing, I decided to go whale watching in a large rubber dinghy. It travelled so fast that the sharp end rose out of the water and soaked the 6 occupants. The good news is that we saw many pilot whales quite close up. A truly wonderful experience. The tour guide was very good, the company was great and the scenery, fabulous, so perhaps it wasn't all bad. It could have had something to do with my age and my two titanium knees perhaps.

Another memorable day was watching the "Running of the Bulls".This takes place in a small village square, where most of the inhabitants and visitors are standing as high up as is humanly possible. In other words, out of the way of the charging bulls.

The bulls are allowed to run through the village, (their horns padded I'm glad to relate), held back by large young strong men on the end of a long rope, the other end which is attached to the bulls neck. This as you can imagine makes the animals rather cross and tetchy. So, they attack anyone or anything they can get at. Here in the Azores the bulls are not injured before or after the run, but this does not stop any unlucky man being attacked and trampled. I think, for me, this was called a local experience. Others might have another name, but I was only a visitor, for the locals it was a tradition which helped the young men prove to the young ladies how brave and virile they were. That was usually before the attack. It was hard to determine if they were still young and virile afterwards, perhaps battered and bruised would be a better description, But......young men will be young men.

2010 SWITZERLAND.

I think I will gloss over this experience. You know when you get older and you are inclined to forget the fact that you have a few things wrong with you, like a heart attack 7 years ago and two knees that are not yours. I forgot these two important facts. The walks arranged were totally beyond my capabilities. I had not read the brochure carefully or taken in what I had seen.
The altitude was the next technical problem. I did make it to the top of the Eiger Mountain only to suffer from the altitude and my heart started to complain rather badly. I was taken under control and rather rapidly taken down to an altitude that my poor little heart could manage. The tour guide was very unsympathetic and told me that I had spoilt everyone's day. Due to all the heaving walking and climbing I developed another problem. My big toe nail dug into the bed of the toe and made any further walking out of the question. This was called PAIN. I spent the rest of the week alone and trying to find something to do and somewhere to go. I managed....... ish. So you see I don't win every time. And there are times when I seem to make a complete idiot of myself.

2011 DALMATION COAST.

The Dalmation cost is beautiful, which I experienced from an 18th century schooner for 8 days. The idea of this trip was to relax, unwind and try to calm down a bit. For me, it was too quiet, with nothing to do all day but watch the sea pass me by. We visited many of the small islands, the weather was good, the food not bad and the company tolerable, The size of my cabin was smaller than my toilet at home. The showers and toilets were on deck. We spent many hours just jumping off the side of the schooner into clear blue water which made snorkelling very easy and pleasant. This trip was not for me, but, until you try these things, how do you know? All I have learnt is that I will not partake in this type of holiday again. So once again, I made a bad mistake. You see I told you that I am not as clever as I thought I was.

Peace and Tranquility

This year things have begun to improve.

ICELANDIC ADVENTURE MAY 22ND TO MAY 28TH 2012.

I flew from Heathrow and after just 2 hours and 55 minutes I landed at Reykjavik Airport, where I was met by my friend Halldor and luckily we recognised each other after 3 years apart. He took me on a fantastic car ride to the unspoilt, highly volatile areas of Iceland where we walked alongside boiling water, thermal pools and sulphur. I casually remarked that I was very thirsty so he drove to the Blue Lagoon thermal pool where fortunately there is a café. After refreshments, the next stop was to a local historic site where I was given a personal guided tour.

On right- Halldor - My Tour Guide.

After many hours of discovering Iceland at the hands of Halldor I was delivered to the Guest House where I would be staying for 6 days. This consisted of a large group of wooden cabins in the woods, a caravan site and or the hardier or foolish types, there were even places to pitch your tent and as the weather was not good I felt very sorry for the inhabitants. My cabin was wonderful. It consisted of 1 large single bed with a bunk above and a smaller single bed. But there was only me, so I decided to sleep in a different bed each night. The facilities were a bathroom with shower and toilet. Radiators in both rooms, kitchen facilities, a fridge, a wardrobe, power points, blinds and curtains and finally a T.V. which didn't work.

The shower was quite something. The overpowering smell of sulphur when you turned the water on was at first a bit of a shock. All the hot water comes naturally from underground and the moment you turn on the taps it is HOT. After I had unpacked and settled into my cabin Halldor picked me up and took me to his house to meet all the family. They have a very large bungalow, well lived in, but, they do have 3 children, a boy aged 17, a girl aged 15 and another girl aged 6. They also have a large black dog and a large black cat. Quite a busy household really which is still suffering from the effects of the last volcanic eruption of 2 years previously. We all sat down together and devoured a very large Pizza, followed by fruit, ice cream and coffee. 2 Years ago Halldor had been in a light aircraft crash and I wanted to hear all about it, plus his other exploits to Greenland, where he had joined a camera crew to get photos and records of seals and Polar bears. He told me that he had tasted raw seal meat and goats testicles. Whilst he was telling me this story he did go a funny colour once or twice. We never stopped talking for 5 hours and it is now 11.00.p.m. and Halldor has to be up very early the next morning as he is a tour guide and will be working all day. I am very lucky, as I have been invited to join the tour free of charge As this is the time of the midnight sun it is still daylight, but I know that sleep will not be a problem. See you in the morning. Wednesday morning. I was up bright and early today, 7.00 a.m to be precise. I had my 'Sulphur shower', followed by the normal ablutions of the day. When all of the above was done and dusted I made my way to the "Camp restaurant for a fabulous breakfast. By 9.30 am Halldor's 17year old son picked me up and drove me to the coach pick up point ready for the day's adventure. It turned out to be a big coach seating 70 people, plus Halldor as the guide for the day. Once again, it's not what you know but who. My day was completely free of charge. We visited the Gullifoss Waterfall and the original Parliament in the hills. We were taken to the formation of the American Plate in all its grandeur. 7 km to the west is the Eurasian tectonic plate, clearly visible with deep fissures. In 2011 there was an earthquake which moved the plates further apart and completely destroyed the tourist path which I had walked on in 2009. It's a very strange feeling and quite difficult to comprehend the magnitude of the earths natural forces. Next on the agenda was a visit to the "Beehive" geyser, which erupts twice in every 5 minutes. The picture I found amusing was to see loads of people around the "Beehive" with their cameras poised waiting for it to blow. But blow it did and you get to know when it's ready. Just before it "blows" a very large bubble of water rises in a dome shape as if by magic, then the cameras get ready as the bubble bursts and shoots hot air and steam some 15-20f eet in the air. What a magnificent sight. The coach then proceeded to drive around the thermal pool area. The ground here is very thin as you can imagine and just our luck the coach got stuck. The big wheels sank into the soft ground and we could not budge an inch. Neither could the traffic coming behind us. What excitement, it could only happen to me. The steam is now erupting out of the fissures and the water temperature is 110 degrees. Some would say, by heck that's hot. Eventually we were all made to leave the coach and try to find some firm ground to stand on whilst a half track pulled the coach out of its predicament. The coach driver felt a bit embarrassed. But we all cheered him up, by saying what an exciting day we had experienced so far. After a much needed lunch we were taken to a fabulous museum run by a gentleman who had started collecting memorabilia at the age of 9. He is now in his retirement years but still running the museum and just loves to personally show his customers around. He asked where we had all come from, most from England, so he sat at his very Old Icelandic piano and whilst we all stood to attention he played the national Anthem just for us. What a memory to take away. The next stop was to see the first Church erected in Iceland, which is still standing. I was then dropped off in Reykjavik to do my own thing for a couple of hours and wait for Halldor to finish his days work. We finally met at the arranged spot, he dropped me off en route to my quiet warm cabin, heated by natural steam and then he went off home to his wife and family in Selfoss. That was the end of yet another tiring but exciting day in Iceland. Thursday morning dawned; it's pouring with rain and blowing a gale. This is known as flaming June. Ooops sorry it is still only May. The plans for today were thus; walk to the Gas station at the end of the road and wait for a coach to pick me up. It was late by 25 minutes, so by now not only am I soaked but bitterly cold. This was another free trip for me as Halldor is guiding a different group of holiday makers. The coach was only a small one today with room for just 20 people. Halldor instructed one of his colleagues to look after this mature English woman as she is one of my friends. AAAH isn't that nice. We were told so many Icelandic folk tales that it is hard to recall even one of them. These old stories are known as Sagas. The coach then proceeded to a glacier, where the more fit ones donned crampons and walked on the glacier for approximately 3 hours. This was not for me; it's very slippery and dangerous. I know when I'm licked and this was one of those occasions. The glacier is also receding very rapidly, helped by all the volcanic ash it has absorbed making it warmer and therefore melting. I am just full of wonderful snippets of information. Whilst the young fit and healthy were doing their bit, I walked with my guide across the area that had been the glacier. It was covered in black ash from the 2010 eruption. I decided to get down on my haunches and investigate. Once you can scrape away some of the ash the ice is still there. This was an unnerving walk to say the least as we are in the path of the next eruption from Hekla. There is a 4-1 chance of eruption as the volcano is growing and the magma chamber is now full. There are posted everywhere alerts to tell you when to run like hell and in which direction. Would it do any good? The total area of Iceland that is black is unbelievable; the farmers have ploughed the fields to put the very fertile ash back into the ground where vegetables can now be planted. Most of the houses in the ash path have been hosed down by the Fire Brigade helping the inhabitants return to some semblance of normality. Fabulous waterfalls were next on the list, Dettifoss, Skaftafell and Gullfoss one of which for the fool hardy, you can actual walk behind which some of the party did. Soaked but happy they all returned alive. The water falls just over 60 feet. The wind was so strong we all got soaked just by the spray. This next phenomenon has to be seen to be believed it is a totally black sand beach where the tide varies up to 12 feet. On our day of the visit the waves were massive. Our guide said that today it was quite calm, cheeky fella, what planet is he on. It's still pouring with rain and the wind is so strong, walking is almost impossible. The beach we finally got blown onto has basalt columns at the base of the cliffs, which glisten when wet. We had the privilege to watch the fulmars, seagulls and puffins land on this massive hillside.

This was not all we saw, Hooper swans, cygnets, ducks of all kinds, so many different varieties of birds, cows, sheep and rams. Some pigs, we are told, are kept but we saw none that day. Once clear of the torrential rain and strong winds we were told what had caused the weird rock shapes which were formed along the coast. They were formed by magma melting either from the top or the side. Nature is a wonder. One area could have been Dirdle Dor in Dorset but without the rough seas. Back on the bus again we saw many ambulances and helicopters. Some tourists in a bus were at the top of the cliff with some standing on the edge when at dusk a large chunk of cliff broke away and fell 40 feet to the beach taking the tourists with it. Luckily, they all lived, one with a broken leg and another with an injury to her back, but not life threatening we were told. They were all lucky to be alive. Iceland is a very volatile country and we as humans have no control over nature. Many more eruptions and earthquakes are due to happen but only God knows when. By the end of the day I was now back in my cabin without Halldor. I am too tired to walk into town to buy something to eat, so I grovelled to the owner of the camp site who made me a sandwich and gave me two biscuits. Wow this is living. I was still peckish so I donned all the waterproof gear and trudged to the garage at the end of the road. Nothing left on sale called food, so I bought a packet of soups, broccoli I think. Back in my cabin the hot soup did the trick. What a fabulous evening meal that was. I've now finished reading my book; the T.V. doesn't work, though even if it did I wouldn't understand anything it said. I'm fed up to the eyebrows with nothing to do and no one to talk to and nowhere to go. Wish you were here. I said to myself Ann; think positive, things can only get better.It was at this point that I decided to telephone Ingibjörg the President of the newly formed U.3.A in Iceland (University of the third age). Being a member of the U3A in England, once my club knew where I was going they suggested I make contact and arrange a get together. We set a date for the next day Friday. Halldor is now on a break so we arranged to meet everyone at the Community Centre in Reykjavik. I felt a bit better now as I had at last achieved something constructive. Once my euphoria had died down I was back to the, I am bored syndrome. So to keep active I put all my needed batteries on charge and then unpacked my rucksack. That took at least 10 minutes. So! What shall I do next? I know, have a nice hot sulphur shower and wash my hair. Well at least it passed the time. See you tomorrow all being well. Friday dawned. The weather is ferocious, with rain, gales, the wind so strong standing upright is almost impossible, very cold. Definitely not suitable light aircraft flying weather, which was one of the things we had planned to do before the week was out. I awoke far too early, so had another shower and hair wash, though why I bothered I'm not sure. The rain would

105

have done the job and the wind would blow my hair dry in 2 seconds. After a very good filling breakfast, Halldor phoned to say he would pick me up at 9.40.a.m to take me to his house after stopping to buy a loaf of bread.He knew I wanted to have some insight into his Greenland expedition and this he did by showing me great pictures on his laptop. He had stayed with the Inuits and spent time with them hunting Minky Whales and killing seals. He was also instructed on how to chew seal skins. He said that was awful along with tasting of the goats testicles, both of which he would not recommend. I then noticed that he had a guitar in the corner of the living room, which was not in a good condition. He does play piano also and very well I might add. I persuaded him to take me to the Town to get his guitar restrung as it had only 4 strings in tact. Whilst this was being done he took me to the revolving restaurant overlooking the town where we had a lovely hot cup of coffee. From here you can see the enormous hot water tank which feeds the city. After the visit to the usual offices we then made our way by car to the community centre to meet members of the U3A Iceland. We spent a very informative 1 and a half hours chatting and relaying stories to each other. They treated us to coffee and snacks. Then to my horror they asked my advice on how to run a U3A. I didn't like to look a twit as I had never run a U3A. I pulled on my vast experience of running other clubs throughout my younger days and finally came up with a few tips which they loved. After saying farewell the Chairman presented me with a flat natural stone with U3A Iceland painted on the surface. She had a wonderful sense of humour. She told me that the stone had cost a LOT OF MONEY, but it was given to keep us all safe and a way of saying "Hello" to the English U3A. I have since given this stone to my club along with best wishes from Iceland U3A. We finally left the Centre with kisses and handshakes all round. They even asked me if I would visit their club and give them one of my talks. That would be some travel expenses, so I think that would not be possible, but I certainly would have loved to do it. Halldor then informed me that there is another pilot on the island who would like to meet me. Things are at last looking better, but still not the weather. Back in the car I was told that we were now going to visit a small town which experienced the strongest earthquake for 100 years. This happened in 2008. The local supermarket was badly hit and proof of this is on video at the shop. A large crevice had opened up in the floor; it was never repaired but covered with glass so that you can see how deep it is whilst standing over the crevice, trying to imagine what it was like on the very day of the earthquake. There was evidence throughout the store of the devastation. It was here we both lost leave of our senses; we paid to go into a mock up house to try to experience a 6.5 earthquake. It was terrifying as this also took place in the pitch dark. We both came out very shaken but not stirred. My Titanium knees didn't like it and neither did Halldor's back injury resulting from his airplane crash. I would hate to be in the real thing. We spoke to some of the locals. Or should I say Halldor did and they reported that new thermals have opened where none were before. The Ravens are no longer nesting on the mountains nearby and some local lakes have completely emptied. They say that these are all signs that another quake is on its way. I have to be honest I suddenly felt just a teeny weensy bit nervous. Tonight I am eating with Halldor's family and after food we will spend the evening with both piano and guitar music. They tried to teach me some Icelandic folk songs but the language for me is impossible. The fun we had that evening wiped out the hours of boredom I had gone through earlier. Whilst Halldor played the piano quietly his dog never made a sound. When he deliberately played loudly the dog howled so loud that the piano could not be heard. He said that he could not play the guitar, but he could, very well, and would you believe the dog stayed silent. Halldor played a wonderful song called, "I'm an Icelandic cowboy on an Icelandic horse". Unfortunately I can't remember the rest even though he sang it in English with a cowboy accent. He was brilliant and very funny, even his 6 year old daughter laughed, so it must have been good. Saturday. Today the weather is a little better, well no rain yet. I even saw the sun for a few fleeting moments. It's still windy, but not quite as violent as the day before. To help me cope with my boredom I have been practising how to say Eyjafjallayokul, the large volcano that erupted in 2010 and bought parts of the world to a standstill. Eureka! I can now say it properly. Today Halldor collected me at about 11.30.a.m in his Range Rover. I foolishly asked, "Why do you need your Range Rover"? Later that day all was revealed. We motored for about 45 minutes stopping once only for a cup of coffee and the usual offices. Due to the fact that Halldor is well known on the island we were allowed a free cup of coffee in the service station staff room. After this stop we drove to his friends' farm, the other pilot I mentioned earlier. They had known each other since their school days together. This friend is, how do you say, a colourful character, much travelled, married a lawyer who he met whilst living in Germany. She must be very clever as she now speaks fluent Icelandic. They have 3 and a half girls, their home and farm property have to be seen to be believed. Rubbish was strewn everywhere, inside and out, derelict huts were in profusion, with dilapidated barns, old disused houses built with grass and mosses just as they had been built in earlier days, both old and new bicycles were scattered throughout the farm area, dogs and horses were roaming freely. He flies a Piper, which is parked in the field and comes into land UNDERNEATH the power lines. You've heard of the expression," Needs some work and modernisation"? This is very true, but they are a lovely family and very happy in their own world. After a light lunch we were taken to the oldest buildings in Iceland which is not open to the public. Halldor's friend had the privilege to be able to visit these buildings and show any of his friends around. One of the oldest remains is dated the 9th Century and thought to be the housing at one time for Monks. Other structures included storehouses, a smithy, a mill house, a cattle shed, a stable, a sheep coral and a tunnel. In their present form they were rebuilt in 1896 and in 1912. The farmstead is built from lava rock from Mount Hekla which just happens to be quite near. Since the mid -20th century the farmhouse has been a part of the National Museum Building Collection. This area of Keldur has a place in history: In the 12th century the manor was owned by no less a famous clan than ODIN. I hope this can bring to your memory the film with Tony Curtis and Kirk Douglas, the latter who played the leader of the Vikings and when in trouble they called for help from ODIN. Iceland has a lot more interesting places to visit, other than active volcanoes. Our next expedition was to some recently excavated man made caves, which dated back to the time of the Vikings. After visiting all these wonderful buildings and caves we dropped Halldor's friend back to his farm to prepare dinner for all his family plus myself and Halldor. We now have the rest of the afternoon to ourselves. I wondered what else I could be taken to see that would blow my mind away. Having driven to Halldor's home we collected his fairly battered 4x4. It took 2 hours to drive to the base of Eyjafjallayokul, through many rivers and uneven terrain of lava and rocks. I very soon realised why we needed the 4x4. Some of the rivers were still quite deep, so we waited until another truck went through O.K. then we felt safe to do the same. We are driving through the plain that was completely flooded in 2010 after the massive eruption. For mile upon mile Halldor steered his vehicle through the fine ash, in some places inches deep. This vista has to be seen to be believed, it was as if I was on another planet, with no human beings in sight and the landscape indescribable. We are now at the base of the glacier that was devastated by the eruption. The magnitude of the glacier is terrifying and awesome as they say in USA. It is forbidden to go too close to the base of the glacier as the whole area is now black quick sands and very dangerous. One step and you would be gone in seconds forever. The worrying thing for me was the fact there were no signs telling tourists of this MINOR PROBLEM. But I was with a very clever local so I knew I was safe. The damage to the glacier is very obvious to see. A vast area of Iceland near

Above - Me flying at 5000ft above Eyjafallayokul.
Left - Glacier formation caused by eruption in 2010. "Spot the Crocodile".

the eruption was flooded due to the melting of part of the glacier.

I am now out of the vehicle and standing below the crater of the famous volcano Eyjafjallayokul. (Pronounced IYER FIAYATLER YAKUL.) Keep practicing, it only took me a week to learn to say this. Have you got it right yet?The weather was hot and windy with fabulous blue skies, but if I'm honest a tad frightening. It took us another 2 hours driving through very rough terrain, in the valley between mountains, glaciers, volcanoes and the rivers, which disturbingly were getting deeper before we were back to civilisation. At last I am back in my cabin and taking a well earned hot sulphur shower, change of clothes and feeling ready to be taken to the friend's farm for dinner. There were 8 of us in total, 4 adults and 3 children with another one on the way. It was organised bedlam, but wonderful. The husband at one time had been a chef amongst many other jobs and just for us he had cooked a whole back bone of lamb. It was the most beautiful tasting piece of lamb I had ever eaten. If I shut my eyes and dream I can still see it, still smell it and still taste it. WONDERFUL. As Halldor is a registered Icelandic tour guide he made the very generous offer to take up to 12 members of my U3A club to either Iceland or Greenland to share with others one of his previous adventures. I really hope some members will take up his offer he is quite some character.

Sunday dawned with unexplainably remarkable weather, just right for the final day of excitement for me, a flight in his light aircraft. I was collected at about 9.00.a.m where he drove to his flying club in Reykjavik. The weather is warm, very sunny, high clouds and no wind to speak of. I couldn't believe my luck; I had waited a whole week for this. I helped take the aircraft out of its hanger, refuelled it, completed all the relevant checks and given clearance for take off. I am now at last being taken on an adventure that one can only dream of. We flew South off the mainland to the Westman islands where a dormant volcano erupted in 1976 at 3.00.p.m. and never stopped for 6 months. Luckily all the inhabitants were evacuated and no one was killed, but one third of the houses are still buried. All the residents 5,000 in total were rescued by the fishing boats in the harbour plus light aircraft from the mainland. The weather was very rough for most small boats which is why aircraft were used. Recently, excavation work has started and the buried houses are being uncovered and even some of the inhabitant's memorabilia is being restored.

Westman Island off the coast of Iceland. "Spot the Elephant".

This is a fishing community and the slow moving lava threatened to close the harbour area leaving everyone cut off, so the local Fire Brigades got together and poured sea water on the lava keeping it away from the harbour entrance successfully for the 6 months. The ingenuity of man never ceases to amaze me. When I realised that my pilot was going to land on this little piece of land, my knees did go a bit week. There were two mountain peaks which he had to fly through the middle of. I think I shut my eyes at this point, but on opening them again saw that we were safely through and now looking for the landing strip. The strip is between two mountain ranges with large rocks at the end of the runway and the harbour on one side, The Island is known for strong cross winds and today was no exception. I think he landed crab wise and I could see the end of the runway getting very near followed by the sea, but being a good pilot we landed perfectly safely. When the eruptions had finally finished the inhabitants returned, where all new houses were built, whilst some were still buried hundreds of feet under lava and ash. In places the ash was over 150 feet deep. To be able to see the whole of the island we booked a taxi and enjoyed the company of a very proud young Icelandic man. After taking of a light lunch on the island we were ready for the next page of the adventure.

We took off and after about 30 minutes were back again over the mainland of Iceland. Suddenly the pilots' mobile phone rang. I don't speak the language so I had no idea not only who it was or what was wanted, but I did see Halldor grin. The gist of the conversation was, "You know my friend and family we had dinner with last night?" I replied, "Yes". "He knows we are flying and has asked us if we would like to drop in for a coffee?" What does one say? Has any one else reading this ever BEEN ASKED TO DROP IN FOR COFFEE WHILST IN A LIGHT AIRCRAFT?

We accepted his invitation and I was told to look out for his farm land and a white barn plus orange cones in a field to denote the grass runway. The coffee tasted rather good and we spent a fun hour exchanging stories, jokes and generally having a good time. But all too soon it became time to leave and get back to the airport. Landing on the grass had not presented itself with any problems whatsoever, but getting airborne was a whole new ball game. Iceland had experienced a lot of heavy rain recently which had made the grass runway, boggy. This problem only became apparent when trying to get airborne. Halldor's friend had asked to join us in the next flight so we now have 3 persons on board. The airplane gets to the end of the grass strip and cannot gain enough speed to get airborne, so take off was immediately aborted. His friend was asked to vacate the aircraft to lighten the load. On the second attempt, the same problem arose, aborted take off. Halldor is now nervous for me and asks me to vacate the aircraft. Before his 3rd try his friend suggested that if this time it was not possible to get airborne, there is a friend in the next field who has a runway on higher ground and that it might be possible to use his runway. Unfortunately the 3rd attempt failed, not enough speed gained to lift off. Halldor now taxis his plane to the next field, after crossing the road, followed by myself and his friend in a van.

The plan is now as follows: Halldor will take off alone to land at another field some 10 miles away and I will be ferried by his friend in the van to find him on this runway waiting for my arrival. Are you following this so far? On my arrival at the strip, there is Halldor in the plane with the engine running, waiting for me to join him. I said a fond farewell to the van driver, ran out to the waiting aircraft which I boarded, strapped in, head set on and away we went, much to the joy of all concerned. We are now flying over Hekla the volcano which erupted in 2002, then on to Eyjafjallayokul which erupted in 2010 bringing the world to a standstill for quite a while, then over the ice cap.

For me, words cannot describe my emotions as we flew at 5,300 feet in minus 30 degrees over crater after crater.

Two Storey House covered in Volcanic Ash - Total depth 60 feet.

A vast area of farmland and beaches are still covered in black ash. The mind boggles at the size of this phenomenon and the devastation it caused when seeing it now was so beautiful and peaceful. The important factor regarding this eruption is that no one lost their lives. According to history no one has been killed due to a volcanic eruption in Iceland for over 1,000 years. After a very memorable 2 and a half hours in the air we finally got back to the airport at Reykjavik, checked out, put the plane to bed and drove for 45 minutes back to the home of Halldor. It wasn't until we landed that I realised Halldor did not look well, he was running a temperature and I think he had flu. At no time did he let on how ill he felt as he wanted to share with me his love of flying in that wonderful wonderland called Iceland. The next day I am up at 5.00 a.m to get to the airport before 7.00 a.m for my flight to Gatwick at 9.00.a.m. This adventure for me was 6 days of wonderful adventure shared with friends and seeing and experiencing wonders of nature. I learnt so much about this wonderful island called Iceland. So don't take my word for it, go and experience for yourself, you will not be disappointed. But one word of advice: take suitable clothing for all 4 seasons.

A DAY TO REMEMBER.

On the 26th March 2013 I was awarded an OBE for my work with and for physically disabled adults including care in the community as a Senior Care attendant.

What an exciting day. The new outfit plus hat was duly purchased and with my 2 sons Ian and Keith 1 Grand Daughter Natalia and Daughter-in-Law Alina we arrived at Buckingham Palace on a very cold windy day for an experience of a life time. After an instruction lesson as to what to do, what to say and what not to say, my name was called. Very nervous, I walked towards Her Majesty curtsying in the correct place. I did become concerned at this point. I have two Titanium knees, what do I do if they creek or give out whilst making my curtsy. Perhaps I could grab her arm and say, "Excuse me Betty could you give me a lift up". Fortunately the curtsy went well without a hiccup. Her Majesty congratulated me on my work and then she asked me to tell her of one particular exploit I had done to raise money. This came as a shock, I was not expecting that. Thinking on my feet I told Her Majesty that I had done a parachute jump dressed as Wonder Woman. Her face was a picture and she asked me to repeat it, which of course I did. She then raised her head towards the beautiful chandelier in the ballroom and laughed out loud. My family who were seated in the front row said, "Oh no Mother's at it again". Her Majesty then extended her hand, which I shook and I knew that was my prompt to GO. I took 3 steps backwards, nearly falling over the carpet, did my final curtsy and walked away with my medal dutifully attached to my outfit. OH BOY did I feel proud.

When my sons asked me, "What did you say to Her Majesty to make her laugh so loudly?" So I told them. Later I was informed by the Palace Guards that I was the only person who made Her Majesty laugh that day.

On arriving back home in West Sussex, my sons posted on Face book."Went to Buck House today with Mum to receive her OBE where she told Her

Majesty about the parachute jump." Of course Her Majesty immediately replied with, "So what, I did one at the Olympic Games". Unfortunately the last sentence was not true, but it made a fun story and we all wished Her Majesty had said just that.

I hope by the time you get to the last chapter you will realise that I have always led a quiet and uneventful life.
I am a very lucky lady. I have two wonderful sons and two equally wonderful Granddaughters who have two great Mums.
So take a leaf out of my book and live your life to the full.
I did and am still doing it, albeit a bit more slowly now.

This is my third book. My first book 'Chance of a Lifetime' was a best seller, here you see a reproduction of the second edition cover. The book tells of some of my exploits, From learning to fly at 50 years old, riding a horse at 60 years old and going on several Wild West adventures. Presently out of print.

I write Odes while I am driving, out walking, just about anywhere. Some are serious but most are about the funnier side of life. If you need to write a 'stern' letter instead write a funny Ode it works. This was my second book,

Pictures on Left; From left - right Natalia, Alina, my Son Ian. My Son Keith, Sharon, Danielle.